→ BAKE

Would you like to learn to be a better baker?

We know that so many people watch *The Great British Bake Off* for the tips and techniques you pick up – not only from the judges, but from watching the bakers too. We wanted to distil that knowledge into a library of cookbooks that are specifically designed to take you from novice to expert baker. Individually, each book covers the skills you will want to perfect so that you can master a particular area of baking – everything from cakes to bread, sweet pastries to pies.

We have chosen recipes that are classics of each type, and grouped them together so that they take you on a progression from 'Easy does it' through 'Needs a little skill' to 'Up for a challenge'. Put together, the full series of books will give you a comprehensive collection of the best recipes, along with all the advice you need to become a better baker.

The triumphs and lessons of the bakers in the tent show us that not everything works every time. But I hope that with these books as your guide, we have given you a head start towards baking it better every time!

Linda Collister
Series Editor

THE GREAT BRITISH BAKE OFF

BAKE OFF ®

—• BAKE IT BETTER •—

CHOCOLATE

Cat Black

HODDER &
STOUGHTON

Contents

BAKE IT BETTER
Baker's Guide

BAKE IT BETTER
Recipes

Easy does it   40

Welcome bakers!

Everybody loves chocolate! It is an ingredient that can make all your baking delicious, and there are 40 classic chocolate recipes in this book.

As well as being great bakes, the recipes have been carefully chosen to introduce you to all the key techniques, such as melting, ganache and tempering, that not only set you up to bake well with chocolate, but which you will find invaluable for all baking.

Start with the 'Easy does it' section and master the basics with recipes like Brownies and Baked White Chocolate Cheesecake. As you grow in confidence you will feel ready to move to the recipes that 'Need a little skill' – a Steamed Chocolate Sponge with Chocolate Custard perhaps, maybe the breakfast favourite, Pains au Chocolat, or an indulgent Baked Chocolate Tart in Chocolate Pastry. The more you bake, the sooner you will be 'Up for a challenge', testing your chocolate skills with the Bûche de Noël or wowing with a centrepiece like the Three Colours Chocolate Cake.

The colour strip on the right-hand side of the page tells you at a glance the level of difficulty of the recipe (from one spoon for easy to three spoons for a challenge), and gives you a helpful checklist of the skills and special equipment you will use.

Before you begin, have a look at the Baker's Guide at the beginning of the book. That will tell you what equipment you need to get started (just a bowl, a spoon and a few baking trays will do!), introduce you to the most important ingredients, and explain some terms and techniques in more detail.

Chocolate has a place in all types of bake, for every time of day. With *Bake It Better: Chocolate* you'll see that it is amazing what you can do with a little chocolate and some know-how. So dive in, and get baking!

HOW TO USE THIS BOOK

SECTION 1: BAKER'S GUIDE
Read this section before you start baking.

The Baker's Guide contains key information on ingredients (pages 11–17), equipment (pages 19–23) and skills (pages 24–43) relevant to the recipes in the book.

Refer back the Baker's Guide when you're baking if you want a refresher on a particular skill. In the recipes the first mention of each skill is highlighted in bold.

SECTION 2: RECIPES
Colour strips on the right-hand side and 1, 2 or 3 spoons show the level of difficulty of the recipe. Within the colour strips you'll find helpful information to help you decide what to bake: Hands-on time; Hands-off time; Baking time; Makes/Serves; Special equipment; Method used; Storage.

Refer back to the Baker's Guide when a skill is highlighted in bold in the recipe if you need a reminder.

Try Something Different options are given where the recipe lends itself to experimenting with other ingredients or decorations.

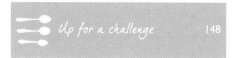

BAKE IT BETTER
Baker's Guide

Ingredients

Baking with chocolate can bring you stunning and varied flavours. It is worth knowing a little about this precious ingredient, and some others that you will use alongside it, in order to make the most of its potential and ensure you produce the most delicious bakes every time. This section also includes some guidelines on things to bear in mind when you are buying, storing and using your ingredients.

BUTTER
Most recipes in this book use **unsalted butter**, which has a lovely rich flavour and gives a more evenly coloured bake because it contains less whey than **salted butters**. Some salted butters also have a stronger taste that can be overpowering in a sweet bake, but if the urge to bake takes you and you only have salted butter, it's really not a big problem; just remember not to add any additional salt.

Wrap butter well and store it in the fridge away from strong flavours, or freeze it for up to a month. Always check the recipe in advance and remove the butter from the fridge in plenty of time so that it is the right consistency for your recipe. If you are going to cream the butter then you will need it to be at room temperature; for pastry you may need it fridge cold. In an emergency you can soften diced butter cubes for a few seconds in the microwave, but take care not to soften it too much – using melted butter instead of softened butter may affect the success of your bake.

CHOCOLATE
Chocolate is a wonderfully versatile ingredient that can be used to achieve many different results, whether to flavour a rich icing for a birthday cake, as chunks in a cookie, or as the star ingredient in a molten, dark chocolate fondant.

The chocolate you use can affect the success of your bake, as well as the flavour, so it is worth choosing carefully. For example, the much higher sugar content in white chocolate means that no added sugar is needed in the White Chocolate Cheesecake (see page 84), which would not be the case in a dark chocolate version of the same recipe. Once you get to know the ways different chocolates behave in recipes you can experiment with the recipes in this book using your favourite types.

One of the most important things to look for in the ingredients list on a bar of chocolate is the percentage. This refers to cocoa solids, which is made up of cocoa mass and cocoa butter and can be anything up to 100 per cent. The remainder of the percentage should only be made up of sugar, milk powder (for a milk chocolate) and possibly lecithin (which helps everything combine together).

To produce the cocoa mass, whole cocoa beans are fermented, dried, roasted and ground. Cocoa butter is the naturally occurring fat in the cocoa bean and usually makes up 40–60 per cent of the bean. Good-quality chocolate won't contain any other fats. When the cocoa mass is refined further (using a process called conching in which the dried and fermented beans are ground between rollers) to make into chocolate, some chocolate makers do add extra cocoa butter to tweak the taste and texture, so its levels will vary, even within chocolates of the same percentage. These differing cocoa butter contents will affect the way the chocolate melts, and so it's worth experimenting with different chocolates to find the ones you most like to work with.

The percentage of cocoa solids is not an indication of the chocolate's quality, but is a guide to its sweetness and intensity of flavour – the lower the percentage the more sugar there is likely to be. It is best to stick roughly to the percentage suggested by a recipe, to get the balance of sweetness right. But you can use a chocolate that is 5 or 10 per cent different if you love it and want to try it in that recipe.

The variety of cocoa, its geographical origin and how it is processed, all play an important part in the final flavour of the chocolate. Tasting different chocolates to find out which you like most is a great way to learn about different varieties. For example, the white Porcelana bean has a simple pure nutty flavour, much like a Macadamia nut, and you can learn to identify these kinds of different qualities as you become more experienced with tasting chocolate.

The top chocolate scientists and connoisseurs have spent the last few years discovering many new varieties, and the list continues to grow. Certain varieties tend to grow well in particular countries and regions – because of climate and geographical preferences – and so it is possible to make some country-wide generalisations: for example, Madagascan chocolate tends to have a red fruit flavour, and much Ecuadorian cacao, particularly Nacional, is also full of fruit flavour notes (see Tasting chocolate, opposite), which can range from cherries to green bananas, with a fresh green herbal quality. Chocolate from Virunga cacao can be wonderfully complex and smoky, Piura from Peru tends to be more delicate, with yellow fruit flavours, and Grenadan cacao produces chocolate

full of lovely round pure chocolate flavour. However, much of the world's cacao comes from West Africa and is from cocoa varieties that tend to be less complex, but it can be rich and deep in flavour when well handled.

As more is learnt about cocoa, and chocolate makers experiment more widely, it can be seen that not only different countries, but also different regions within countries, and even different plantations, can result in chocolate with very different characteristics. Chocolate makers in Vietnam are discovering a world of different flavours across that one country. Like the study of wine, this is an exciting area of taste, one that is just opening up to us.

Tasting chocolate

As we have just seen, chocolate is an ingredient whose flavours can vary enormously, with the cocoa variety and the many stages of processing each influencing the final chocolate. To appreciate its potential, and to fully recognise its flavour profile (the many flavours within a particular chocolate), it is important to taste it fully and properly. Then you will be able to make informed choices about which chocolates to use in your recipes with which flavour pairings – and, of course, to find and realise which chocolates you most like!

The key is to eat chocolate slowly, allowing it to melt fully in the mouth. This allows time for the cocoa butter in the chocolate to release all the flavours where your taste buds and nose can experience them. If you simply chew and swallow those flavours will be released after the chocolate has reached your throat or stomach, and you will only experience the first flavours, or top notes, of the chocolate (which tend to be the most astringent), and its tannins.

Chocolate has top notes, middle notes and base notes, which can take you on a complete flavour journey from start to finish. Typically the top notes (the first to hit your palate) are the brightest – so green, herbal or bright fruit flavours. The middle notes will be sweetest – toffee, caramel, dried fruit and spicy flavours may come in. The final flavours will be the darkest – cocoa or coffee, and any smokiness. These flavour notes will vary between cocoa varieties, growing locations, chocolate makers, and even between individual harvests or batches of chocolate. Of course there will be times when you just want to munch on some chocolate and won't need to pay attention to these considerations. But with good-quality chocolate it is worth taking the time to taste fully, to make the most of the chocolate, both to eat and as an ingredient.

How to taste chocolate

1. Look at the chocolate and make a note of what colour it is. The colour can give you information about the chocolate. For example, a very light colour in a high-percentage chocolate may indicate rare white Porcelana beans, or a very dark colour might give an indication that the cocoa beans have been over-roasted or burnt.
2. Smell the chocolate. As so much of the flavour of chocolate is in fine aromas, this can be a first idea of how the chocolate may taste.
3. Break the chocolate. Does it snap? Is it well tempered and well presented? This can be an indication of quality or how well the chocolate has been stored.
4. Put the chocolate in your mouth and allow it to melt fully. If it is a thick piece, or particularly cold, you may wish to break it up a little with your teeth, but then let it

fully melt before swallowing.
5. As the chocolate melts make a note of the progression of flavours you experience. You could make notes and build up a library of your knowledge to use when thinking of flavour pairing. Certainly make a note of which chocolates you like, so you can buy them again later.
6. Notice the aftertaste. A fine chocolate will not only have an interesting flavour journey but a long aftertaste.

Choosing chocolate for a recipe

Always use the best quality chocolate that you can, as the quality of ingredients will have a big effect on the outcome of your bake. Start by reading the instructions in the recipe as to the type and percentage of chocolate that is recommended. Then use your experience **tasting** chocolate to make your choice within that. Consider the amount of chocolate in a recipe: if you are making a very rich Dark Chocolate Ganache tart (see page 92), for example, using a chocolate with brighter, fruity flavours will make the tart lighter to eat than a very intense chocolate with deep flavours. It's worth understanding how certain flavour notes pair well with added ingredients, such as raspberries with Madagascan chocolate, which tends to have red fruity notes. (See opposite for more information on how geographical origin can affect the taste.) Many of the recipes in this book have suggestions to help you choose the right chocolate, but there is much more to be learnt and tasted, so do experiment.

Types of chocolate

Dark chocolate should only contain cocoa solids and sugar, although it may contain lecithin, a natural emulsifier that can make the chocolate easier to melt and work with. Dark chocolate is usually between 60 and 100 per cent cocoa solids and is the first choice for most chocolate recipes, such as a flourless chocolate cake or brownie, because it has the purest chocolate taste. It also sets with a firmer texture (because of its lower fat content) and achieves a better shine than milk or white chocolate, which is good to bear in mind when making chocolate shards or other decorations.

Milk chocolate has a creamier taste and texture, as milk powder is added to its other ingredients, cocoa solids and sugar. The cocoa content is traditionally lower than in dark chocolate. The requirement for milk chocolate in Europe is that it has more than 25 per cent cocoa mass; but aim for 35 per cent and above if you can as it will have a much fuller flavour.

High-percentage milk chocolate is also now available and has the intense detailed cocoa flavour of dark chocolate, combined with the mellowness of milk chocolate.

White chocolate doesn't have any cocoa mass. It contains cocoa butter, milk and sugar, and is traditionally flavoured with vanilla, although you can also now get white chocolate without vanilla, which has a pure, creamy taste.

White chocolate is great for bakers as it has the physical properties of chocolate, but without its taste, which means that it can be combined with a much wider range of flavours than dark chocolate.

Ensure that the white chocolate you use contains no fats other than cocoa butter. Look for chocolate which is at least 35 per cent cocoa butter for a fine quality white chocolate.

Cocoa powder is an unsweetened powder made from cocoa beans, with some of the cocoa butter removed. It is intense in flavour, and adds an excellent chocolate taste to recipes that would not work so well with melted chocolate, such as sweet pastry or light sponge cakes.

Cocoa nibs are small shards of shelled, roasted cocoa beans. As such they are unsweetened, and at 100 per cent cocoa, have a very intense flavour, like cocoa powder. They are an excellent way to bring flavour and texture to both sweet and savoury dishes, such as the Cocoa Nib Soda Bread on page 58.

Hot chocolate powder is a preparation sold to make it easy to make a hot chocolate drink. It has powdered milk and sugar already added to it, so it is very important not to confuse it with pure cocoa powder when buying or assembling ingredients for your recipes as it will affect the success of your bake. It does have its uses in some baking though, and can be a handy store cupboard ingredient (see Hot Chocolate Cupcakes, page 54). However, the best hot chocolate drink is made simply by stirring chopped chocolate into hot milk or water until it dissolves.

Storing chocolate

There are two main things to consider when storing chocolate: temperature and proximity to other foods or smells. Chocolate will readily absorb outside aromas, so it is important to keep it in an airtight container or wrapping, so that it doesn't take on the flavours of strong smelling foods nearby. Chocolate needs to be kept relatively cool too, to avoid the risk of it melting. If it melts it will come 'out of temper', which means it will lose its shine and desirable snap. It will also become streaky or show creamy coloured 'bloom' and remain soft. This doesn't mean it has gone bad, but it will remain that way unless it is tempered again.

The fridge is not ideal for chocolate, as it is a moist atmosphere that can spoil the chocolate; 12–16°C (54–60°F) is optimum and many chocolate connoisseurs actually use a wine fridge to store their chocolate. An airtight container in a cool dry place is perfect too. Remember to check with the chocolatier or on the packaging of the chocolate for use-by dates. Most plain bars will last for many months, but filled chocolates and fresh ganaches may have a shelf life of only a week or so.

CREAM
Always use the cream recommended in the recipe – the fat content varies significantly and can have a huge effect on your bake. **Single cream** has at least 18 per cent butterfat and is good for pouring and certain sauces, but it is not suitable for whipping. **Double cream** has at least 48 per cent butterfat and whips well when thoroughly chilled. Don't use the extra-thick double cream labelled 'for spooning' as you won't be able to whip it; nor is it suitable for making ganache. **Whipping cream** does exactly what it says on the tub. It has at least 35 per cent butterfat and for best results, chill it thoroughly before whipping. If you need to use whipping cream and can only find double cream you can make whipping cream by mixing 3 parts double cream with 1 part full-fat milk.

EGGS
All the recipes in this book use medium-sized eggs (about 62–65g each). When it comes to eggs, size really is important; using a different-sized egg may affect the success of your recipe, by altering the texture and moisture of cake batter, cookie dough or pastry. Meringues, soufflés and custards also rely on specific ratios of egg white or egg yolk with other ingredients. Store eggs in the fridge, pointed-side down, as this protects the yolk from drying out and spoiling. Keep them in the box they came in and in the cooler body of the fridge, not the door, and use by the best before date on the box. Many of the recipes call for either egg whites or egg yolks; you can keep both, covered, in the fridge for 3–4 days. Spare egg whites freeze well for up to a month – just make sure they're thoroughly defrosted before use. (A good tip is to mark the quantity and date on the container.) Egg yolks should not be frozen. Eggs should be used at room temperature as they will produce a greater volume when beaten, so bring them out of the fridge 30–60 minutes before you want to use them. If you forget to do this you can gently warm them up in a bowl of lukewarm water for 10 minutes.

EXTRACTS AND FLAVOURINGS
Chocolate, and recipes that use chocolate, can be flavoured in any number of ways, from infusing hot cream to make a ganache (see pages 26–27) to simply adding ground spices to cakes and biscuits.

Vanilla extract is now widely available – try to avoid the cheaper essence, which is a chemical, rather than natural flavouring. Ground and whole **spices** should be measured carefully and kept in screw-topped jars rather than open packs. Use them when they are fresh and within a few months of opening. **Coffee** flavour can be added to recipes using instant coffee granules and works wonderfully with chocolate, as in the Coffee Bourbons (page 60). Other flavours that work well with chocolate include fresh **mint**, grated **orange or lemon zest** (use unwaxed lemons) and even fresh **chilli**.

FLOUR

Poor-quality flour or past-its-best flour can really affect the final taste and texture of your bake, so only use flour when it's fresh and store it correctly between uses: keep opened packs of flour in tightly sealed storage jars, plastic food boxes or plastic food bags to stop it getting damp. Don't add new flour to old storage jars, and aim to use it within a month of opening or by its best before date.

Wheat flours are the most commonly used flours in baking and most of the recipes in this book call for **plain flour**, which is simply flour with nothing else added. It gives a lovely short texture to pastry and, when combined with a raising agent such as baking powder, gives a lightness to biscuits and cakes. **Self-raising flour** is made from plain flour to which baking powder has been added so that the mixture expands and rises in the oven. You can make your own self-raising flour by adding 4 teaspoons of baking powder to every 225g plain flour. **Ground almonds** work well with chocolate cakes, adding texture and moistness – and they are also gluten-free – but they can go rancid quite quickly so it's best to store them in an airtight container and make sure to use them before their best before date.

There are lots of **gluten-free flours** readily available now. They are usually made from a combination of rice, potato, tapioca, maize, chickpea, broad bean, white sorghum or buckwheat flours. They can vary a lot in terms of texture and taste so try out different brands to see which is your favourite. A few are specially made for cake-making and so can be substituted fairly easily, although some do suggest adding xanthan gum which can help the structure of the bake. Sometimes you may need a bit less liquid too, so always make sure you follow the instructions on the packet and experiment to get the desired results. (It's also worth checking whether your baking powder is gluten-free.)

MARGARINES AND SPREADS

These are based on vegetable oils, with added salt and flavourings. Some are made specifically for baking but are not used for the recipes in this book. Where butter is specified it is best not to substitute with margarine or a spread as the flavour will differ, as will the water content, so they are unlikely to result in a successful bake.

NUTS

Nuts are a natural partner for chocolate, with all the different varieties working well with it in different ways. Nuts have distinct and varied flavours and textures, so the type of nut you use will be important to your bake. A recipe will usually say if you can try it with different varieties. Some nuts are oilier than others, which can affect the baking time and the textures. Their consistency, whether whole, chopped or ground, is also crucial to baking success, so check the recipe to make sure you are using what is needed. For example, **walnuts** and **pecans**, which are softer on the bite, go well whole in cakes and muffins, where whole **almonds** or **hazelnuts** would be too hard. Roasting nuts increases their flavour, but they burn easily, so watch them carefully. When using ground nuts, grinding them yourself in a food processor will always result in a better flavour than buying them ready ground. Nuts can quickly turn rancid and bitter, so store them in a screw-topped jar or airtight container in a cool, dark spot and use before their best before date.

SALT

Salt is an unexpected, but essential, ingredient in much sweet baking. While the resulting bakes do not taste salty, it rounds out the flavours and they would taste bland without it. For the most part fine table salt is perfect for your baking – it is fine enough to incorporate quickly into your mixtures. When making salted caramelised nuts or salted caramels, or decorating chocolates or bakes with a few salt crystals, you may want to experiment with sea salt flakes, which have a fine flavour and an attractive appearance. However don't use rock salt, as the crystals are too thick to absorb well into mixtures or when eaten and you are left with large gritty pieces.

SUGAR

Always use the type of sugar recommended in the recipe. They combine with other ingredients in slightly different ways, which can affect how your final bake will turn out.

The fine texture of **caster sugar** makes it ideal for most general baking, as it incorporates easily into your mixtures and combines well with butter. **Golden caster sugar** is less refined, retaining the molasses of the sugar cane. It is not so easily combined so techniques such as creaming will take longer. It has a richer colour and flavour. **Granulated sugar** takes longer to dissolve and can leave a speckled appearance on top of your bakes.

The fine powdered texture of **icing sugar** allows it to melt instantly into mixtures such as sweet pastry or icing, or where a sugar with no granular texture is needed.

Light and dark muscovado sugars add a stronger caramel taste, and are used when a warmer butterscotch or caramel taste is wanted. They can form into lumps during storage, so you'll need to sift or press the lumps out before using.

Equipment

You don't need a lot of complicated equipment to get started baking, and there will be recipes in this book that can be made with just a bowl, a wooden spoon and whatever baking tin you already have. If you want to start tackling more complex recipes, you may need a few extra bits of equipment. Do check each recipe before you start, as then you will know what you need to complete it. Here is a guide to some of the basic kit, and some of the specialist equipment you might want to experiment with.

ACETATE SHEET
This clear sheet is used in creating tempered chocolate decorations. Its flexibility allows the chocolate to be moved and manipulated and its shiny surface imparts a high sheen to the chocolate.

BAKING BEANS
Ceramic baking beans are used when blind baking (see pages 37–8) to keep pastry bases flat and the sides upright. You can always set aside a jar of uncooked rice or dried beans to use instead, but ceramic beans are generally re-usable over a longer period of time.

BAKING PAPER AND LINERS
Lining papers make it easier to remove your bake from the tin once it's cooked. **Non-stick baking paper** is suitable for most purposes and is good for delicate mixtures; it is also used to line uncooked pastry cases when baking blind (see pages 37–8). **Parchment-lined foil** is heavier and can be folded to make a strong cover for a steamed pudding. **Liners and discs** for lining the bases of tins will save you time and effort if you bake dozens of cakes,

and are available from most supermarkets. **Re-usable silicone liners** are excellent for lining baking sheets and can be cut to fit other tins you use regularly. **Greaseproof paper** is best kept for wrapping cooked food as it is water resistant, but its waxy coating doesn't stand up well to heating and your cakes may stick to it.

BAKING SHEETS AND TRAYS
You will need strong baking sheets that won't buckle and twist in the oven and it's worth having two or three to hand so that you can complete and bake a whole recipe at once, without having to wait for them to become available. These are used most for cookies or small bakes such as Pains au Chocolat (see page 126). Baking sheets with only one raised edge make it easy to slide a palette knife under delicate biscuits. **Traybake tins** are square or rectangular with sides that are about 4cm high. They are endlessly versatile and are used in this book for making Brownies, Blueberry Blondies and Cocoa Nib and Chocolate Chip Granola Bars (see pages 66, 68 and 64). A 23cm square tin is used for most of the traybakes in this book. **Swiss roll tins** are rectangular with shallow sides that are about 2cm high. The most useful sizes are 20 × 30cm and 23 × 33cm. These are needed to make rolled cakes such as the Bûche de Noël (see page 154).

BOWLS
It is useful to have a variety of bowls, of different types and sizes. There are pros and cons to the different types. **Heatproof glass** bowls are a good all-purpose choice for mixing, whisking and melting chocolate – make sure you have one that fits snugly over a pan, leaving enough room below to

simmer some water without it touching the bowl. **Stainless steel** bowls are unbreakable and dishwasher-proof, but they won't go in the microwave. **Ceramic** bowls are pretty and can go in the dishwasher but can break quite easily and can be heavy. **Plastic** are all-purpose and cheap, and ones with rubber bases are non-slip. (You can solve the slip issue by placing a damp cloth underneath any bowl.) **Anodised aluminium** bowls are very durable and will last a lifetime but, again, they're no good for the microwave.

CAKE TINS

It is very important to use the tin that's specified in the recipe. The quantities and baking time have been calculated to work with that particular cake tin and your bake won't turn out the way it's supposed to if you use a different one. (It will specify in the recipe if the bake can work well in a different tin.) A really solid, heavy-duty tin will last forever, withstand repeated baking without scorching or warping, and stay rust-free if you take care of it, which means washing and drying it thoroughly after use. Heavy-duty metal cake tins are probably the most reliable and durable, but there are other options such as heavy aluminium, glass, ceramic or silicone. Avoid flimsy non-stick tins as they will quickly lose their coating. Never use a tin that has started to shed its coating as bits of it could end up in your bake. If you opt for silicone moulds, a baking sheet underneath will help stabilise the mould before you pour in the mixture, and when you're transferring it to the oven.

Deep round cake tins are good for most cakes; loose-bottomed cake tins make it far easier to remove your cake when baked.

This is particularly true with chocolate cakes, which can be very rich and damp, and so fragile to handle or prone to sticking to the tin. Tins of 20cm and 23cm diameter are those you will probably use most.

Loaf tins can be used for cakes like the Chocolate Loaf Cake (page 70). The 450g (about 19 × 12.5 × 7.5cm) and 900g (about 26 × 12.5 × 7.5cm) tins are the most commonly used sizes.

Muffin tins, usually with 12 holes, make it possible to bake individual muffins and cupcakes. The recipes in this book are made with full size muffin tins and cases.

Sandwich tins are extremely useful when making layer cakes such as the Three Colours Chocolate Cake (page 168), as they help you achieve identical layers.

Specialist tins are useful if you want to bake recipes such as the Financiers, for which you'll need a financier mould tray. Recipes such as the Cinnamon and Chocolate Tiger Bundt Cake (page 72) also use specialist tins but it is often possible to use standard tins instead (see the individual recipe methods for instructions on adapting to regular tins).

Springclip tins have a spring release, a base that clamps in place when the clip is fastened and a deep metal ring which lifts off when unfastened. These are really helpful when making cheesecakes and fragile cakes such as the Chocolate Truffle Cake and the Flourless Chocolate Cake (see pages 74 and 82). They come in many sizes, but 20.5cm and 22–23cm tins are the most useful.

Tart tins are ideal for cooking your tarts and quiches and can be large or small. A loose-bottomed tart tin will make it much easier to remove your finished bake.

COOLING RACKS
Wire cooling racks with legs allow the air to circulate underneath your cooling bakes, preventing condensation and the dreaded 'soggy bottom'. If needs be, you can improvise with a clean grill-pan rack, but the finer wires on a cooling rack are more effective.

FOOD-PROCESSOR
A food-processor makes light work of chopping and blending. Although not essential for most bakes, they are very useful for making pastry, as they allow the mixture to be handled very briefly and unlike fingers the metal blades stay cool while processing. However, a food-processor is essential for the fine grinding of nuts and praline.

MEASURING JUG
Pick a heat-resistant and microwave-safe jug that has both metric and imperial measures, starting from 50ml if you can find one, otherwise 100ml, and going up to 2 litres. A small jug or cup that measures from 1 teaspoon (5ml) up to 4 tablespoons (60ml) is a very useful extra. You can also get measuring jugs with cup measurements – useful if you bake a lot of North American recipes.

MEASURING SPOONS
Everyday teaspoons, dessertspoons and tablespoons vary enormously in size so you shouldn't use them to measure ingredients. Baking is such an exact science that it's worth investing in proper measuring spoons for small amounts of liquids and dry ingredients (such as baking powder, spices, salt and sugar), ranging from ⅛ teaspoon to 1½ tablespoons. Go for spoons with narrow ends that will fit into fiddly spice jars. Unless the recipe says otherwise, all spoon measures in these recipes are level – skim off the excess with a finger or the back of a knife.

METAL SPATULA
A flat wide metal spatula or slice is the best tool for lifting cookies and other pastries from the baking sheet once cooked. With tricky recipes it would be very hard to do it without one (see Florentines, page 100).

MICROWAVE
A microwave oven can be a very useful tool for home chocolate work as it can be used for **melting** and **tempering** chocolate. When working with chocolate, use the microwave in very short bursts and stir after each burst of heat, to prevent overheating or hot spots. You can also use the microwave to soften butter and reheat sauces and custard. Just be careful not to overheat.

MOULDS
Chocolate moulds come in an infinite variety of shapes and sizes. Professional polycarbonate moulds are the most expensive and they have a fine mirror-like surface, which allows you to achieve a really high shine. You can get cheaper silicone and plastic moulds but you will struggle to get such a high shine. Silicone moulds are useful if you want to make solid moulded chocolates that are easy to turn out (see the White Chocolate Easter Egg and Moulded Chocolates on page 142). You can also use other objects, such as fresh leaves, to create chocolate shapes (see Bûche de Noël, page 154).

OVEN THERMOMETER

Baking requires accuracy and as the internal thermostats of ovens vary, you may want to invest in an oven thermometer to make sure it is the correct temperature – and to identify any hotter or cooler spots.

PALETTE KNIFE

A flat metal palette knife makes it easier to spread icings and mousse in even strokes, as well as to lift biscuits and other bakes from baking sheets.

PASTRY BRUSH

Pastry brushes are useful for brushing on glazes, greasing tins with melted butter, or painting tempered chocolate in fine layers. Be sure to get one that is dishwasher safe and heatproof, and watch out for shedding hairs that might end up in your bake.

PIPING BAGS

Disposable plastic piping bags in various sizes are available from most supermarkets. Generally the ones with the non-slip exteriors are easiest to use. You can also find reusable **nylon piping bags** from specialist shops and cake-decorating suppliers. They have a little more weight and strength to them and don't have seams for the mixtures to leak through. Most can be rinsed and then washed inside out in very hot water. Always make sure they are completely dry before putting them away. It is often easiest when piping molten chocolate or ganache to use a disposable bag with the end snipped off to the right size.

PIPING NOZZLES

These conical tubes fit into the end of piping bags and are available in scores of shapes and sizes. The best value are sets that provide a reusable bag plus a set of stainless steel nozzles, either just the small size for decorating or an all-round set that includes large (1.5–2cm), plain and star nozzles.

ROLLING PIN

A good rolling pin should be heavy and at least 6cm wide and long enough to roll pastry to fill your widest tart tin. Treat it carefully; don't use it for crushing nuts or anything else, as once the surface is pitted it will no longer roll out your dough into a smooth unblemished surface.

SCALES

Baking is really a science, so it pays to be accurate if you want perfect results every time. As you'll be dealing with small quantities, **digital** scales are preferable to **spring** or **balance** scales as they are much more precise and can weigh ingredients that are as little as 1 gram. You can see the weight easily at a glance and add multiple items to one bowl simply by resetting the balance to zero after adding each ingredient. Always keep a spare battery on standby.

SCRAPER

You will need a scraper when working with tempered chocolate. It is useful for levelling molten chocolate, spreading fine layers of the chocolate and cleaning up your surfaces afterwards. You can also use it to make curls and ruffles to decorate your bakes.

SIEVE

Essential for removing lumps from icing sugar and other ingredients, and to bring air into mixtures. A stainless steel wire sieve with a large bowl is the most versatile and should last longer than plastic. A smaller tea strainer-sized sieve is also a good piece of kit to have, for dusting cakes and bakes with icing sugar and cocoa powder.

SKEWER

A metal skewer is handy to insert into cakes to check they are done. You can use a knife, but a skewer will leave a smaller hole.

SPATULAS

Flexibility is key here. You want a good-sized rubber or plastic spatula that's heat-resistant for mixing ingredients together, cleaning out bowls and spreading mixtures. A smaller one is useful for fiddly amounts.

THERMOMETER

A good kitchen thermometer is essential when tempering chocolate and making caramels. You need one with a long metal probe to reach down into your mixture. Digital thermometers are accurate and fine tuned for the kind of small temperature changes you need to register.

TIMER

It's all too easy to forget when the bakes went into the oven – we've all done it – so switch a timer on to avoid burnt biscuits, chocolate fondants that don't have molten centres and cakes that are not as moist as they should be. Go for one that has seconds as well as minutes – and a loud ring. Set it for 5 minutes less than the suggested time in your recipe, especially if you are unsure of your oven temperature – you can always increase the baking time if needed.

WHISKS AND MIXERS

These range from the most basic, which means the baker has to do the energetic whisking, to free-standing food mixers that do all the hard work for you.

Wire whisks can be balloon-shaped or flat. A sturdy hand-held wire whisk with an easy-grip handle that fits your hand is ideal for whisking mixtures on and off the heat.

Hand-held rotary whisks have two beaters in a metal frame, which are turned by hand. They're perfect for whisking egg whites, whisking mixtures over heat (no trailing leads) and whisking out lumps in batters.

Hand-held electric whisks are more expensive, but much more powerful and can be used for most general mixing. Look for models with a set of attachments and a retractable cord for easy storage.

Free-standing electric mixers really do save time and energy if you do a lot of baking. A large free-standing model with attachments for beating, whisking and making dough is a great investment. If possible, buy an extra bowl, as it helps when making bakes with multiple elements. Large mixers do all the beating and whisking for you, so you will get more volume into your meringues and whisked egg mixtures in a much shorter time, and they are great for batch-baking. They do take up space though, so they're not ideal for a small kitchen – a hand-held electric whisk would suit better, and almost all whisking can be done with a hand-held rotary whisk.

WOODEN SPOONS

The unsung heroes of the kitchen – they're heat-resistant, won't scratch non-stick pans and are ideal for stirring and beating. Keep a collection of different shapes and sizes. Keep ones for baking separate from those used for savoury cooking, as the wood is porous and will absorb strong flavours.

Skills

Now that you have all your ingredients and equipment ready, you're ready to get baking with chocolate. This section covers all the key information about handling chocolate, as well as some essential baking skills that you'll need, from baking your first batch of chocolate cookies to creating spectacular showstoppers. It's worth reading it at least once, so you have some guidance and can enjoy your baking safe in the knowledge that you'll be happy with the end results. All the recipes in the book tell you exactly what you need to do step-by-step, but you'll notice that some of the terms are highlighted in bold, which means you can refer back to this section if you want a bit more detail, or to refresh your memory.

THE KEY CHOCOLATE TECHNIQUES

This section contains all the essential know-how for working with chocolate.

MELTING CHOCOLATE

Chocolate melts at body heat, which is why it has that glorious melt-in-the-mouth quality. It melts into a smooth liquid at a low enough temperature to be incorporated into cakes, bakes, sauces and puddings before or during cooking, which is what makes it such a fantastic and versatile ingredient.

Melting chocolate isn't tricky, but it needs a little preparation and patience. Finely chop your chocolate to ensure it melts quickly and evenly, or use good-quality chocolate chips. (These are not to be confused with the chocolate chips you might use when making cookies, which are often made from chocolate that is lower quality and with a higher sugar and lower cocoa content.) Many good chocolates are made into buttons or 'pistoles' for chefs to use more easily – you can buy these from specialist suppliers and online.

When melting white chocolate, try not to overheat it – white chocolate pieces may keep their shape even when the chocolate is melted because of its much higher fat and sugar content.

If you do happen to overheat or scorch your chocolate as you melt it, it will become greasy, grainy (known as 'seizing') and unusable, so you'll have to start again. Dark chocolate with a very high cocoa solid content (more than 70 per cent) and sugary white chocolate are more delicate and prone to overheating and seizing. Many recipes in this book will ask you to melt the chocolate in the heat from other ingredients, which shows you just how little heat is needed.

How to melt chocolate in a bain-marie
This is the traditional way of melting chocolate, and works whether you are melting chocolate on its own or with other ingredients such as brandy or milk. It allows chocolate to melt without coming into direct contact with the source of heat, which may cause it to burn. A good tip to avoid overheating chocolate is always to remove the pan from the heat, and then the bowl from the pan, before the chocolate has fully melted. The last pieces will melt in the residual warmth of the bowl.

1. Put the chocolate into a heatproof bowl that fits snugly over a pan of gently simmering water – the bottom of the bowl should not come into contact with the water below or the chocolate may scorch and burn and become unusable.
2. Leave the chocolate to melt in the heat from the water for a couple of minutes and then gently stir with a spoon or spatula until it is completely smooth (*see photo, right*). It is ready to use as melted chocolate as soon as it is smooth and liquid – around 30°C (86°F).
Learn with: Chocolate Truffle Cake (page 74), Chocolate Soufflé (page 80) and Chocolate Éclairs (page 110)

How to melt chocolate in a microwave
Melting chocolate in a microwave is an alternative to using a bain-marie and the two methods are interchangeable, as long as you are confident using a microwave. It can be harder to keep an eye on the chocolate in the microwave so always melt it in short bursts to avoid overheating.
1. Put the chocolate in a heatproof bowl and place it in the microwave.
2. Heat the chocolate on the lowest heat for a few seconds only, before taking it out to check. You do not want any part of

the chocolate to become too hot, or it will scorch and spoil.

3. Using a rubber spatula stir the chocolate between each short burst of heat until it starts to melt.

4. When the chocolate is roughly two-thirds melted stop using the microwave and stir the chocolate to allow the remaining chocolate to melt in the residual heat of the bowl.

How to melt chocolate in a pan
If you have a substantial amount of another ingredient to melt with your chocolate, such as butter, there is less risk of it burning so you can melt it in a saucepan. Simply place the chocolate and other ingredients in a pan and set it directly over a low heat, stirring once or twice and watching it very carefully. *Learn with: Brownies (page 66), Blueberry Blondies (page 68) and Chocolate Loaf Cake (page 70)*

CHOCOLATE GANACHE
Ganache is the soft chocolate preparation that traditionally forms the centre of truffles. It is also used in many areas of patisserie, for filling, icing and covering fine chocolate creations. A classic ganache is made with chocolate, cream and sometimes butter. Recently, innovative chefs have developed a water ganache, which lets the purer flavours of the chocolate come through without being diluted by the addition of cream.

How to make a classic ganache
1. Ensure the chocolate is broken into small even pieces, and put it into a heatproof bowl (*see photo, left*).

2. Next put the cream in a pan and bring just up to the boil. Then let it sit for a minute to cool a little. You don't want it scalding hot;

neither do you want it to lose so much heat that it will not melt the chocolate.

3. Pour the hot cream over the chocolate and stir in small circular actions to gradually incorporate all the chocolate into the cream to make the ganache (*see photo, right*).

4. Then add the butter (if using), piece by piece and beat the ganache until it is all smoothly amalgamated.

5. At this point pour the ganache into your mould to set before cutting or rolling for truffles, or set it aside at room temperature if you will be using it piped or spread.

Learn with: Simple Chocolate Truffles (page 52), Dark Chocolate Ganache Tart (page 92) and Macarons with Cardamom Ganache (page 138)

How to make a water ganache

1. Ensure the chocolate is broken into small pieces, and put it into a heatproof bowl.

2. Next heat the water, or any other water-based liquid that you are using (orange juice, tea etc) in a pan and bring just up to steaming point. Then let it sit for a minute to cool a little. You don't want it scalding hot; neither do you want it to lose so much heat that it will not melt the chocolate.

3. Pour the hot liquid over the chocolate and stir to melt, gradually incorporating all the chocolate into the liquid to make a ganache.

4. At this point pour the ganache into your mould to set before cutting or rolling for truffles, or set it aside at room temperature if you will be using it piped or spread.

Learn with: Box of Chocolates/Earl Grey truffles (page 160)

How to cut ganache

To turn ganache into truffles you need to shape it into small pieces. Then the truffles can be covered with tempered chocolate

(see How to enrobe, page 32) or simply dusted or rolled in cocoa powder or other ingredients to form your finished chocolates.

1. To create square truffles, or ganache rectangles for enrobing, you will need to have set and chilled your ganache in a square or rectangular mould, or cake tin.

2. Turn the ganache out onto a clean cutting board covered in baking paper.

3. You will need a large sharp knife with a deep blade. Warm the knife in hot water, and keep a towel nearby to wipe it dry after each time you dip it in the water.

4. Cut the ganache with the warmed knife into squares or rectangles the correct size for your recipe (*see photo, left*).

5. Place each piece of cut ganache onto a clean sheet of baking paper or directly into its coating, to ensure that it remains separate from the rest of the ganache and doesn't stick.

6. If you are not going on to enrobe the truffles you will need to keep them chilled, as they will soften quickly at room temperature.

Learn with: Simple Chocolate Truffles (page 52) and Fresh Mint Ganache Truffles in Dark Chocolate (page 118)

How to roll ganache

If you don't want square or rectangle truffles, you can roll your ganache into small balls using your hands. It can also be easier to coat balls (rather than blocks) in different flavourings, such as nuts, or in cocoa powder or icing sugar.

1. Place the bowl in which you made your ganache in the fridge to firm up.

2. Take it out of the fridge when set – if it is too hard to work with you may need to leave it at room temperature for a few minutes.

3. Dust your hands with cocoa powder and

reapply it regularly, or wear fine disposable kitchen gloves.

4. Using a small spoon, scoop rough balls of ganache out of the bowl.

5. Roll the balls between your palms to mould them into smooth, even balls (*see photo, right*). You will need to work quickly as the ganache will soften up in the warmth of your hands and become more difficult to shape.

6. Place each ball onto a clean sheet of baking paper, on a plate or directly into its coating, to ensure that it doesn't stick to anything. If you are not going on to enrobe the truffles you will need to keep them chilled, as they will soften quickly at room temperature.

Learn with: Bûche de Noël (page 154)

TEMPERING CHOCOLATE

Tempering is an essential chocolate skill to master. The process of tempering gives chocolate its most stable structure, meaning that it can be moulded, can hold fine detail, will hold a great shine and will give you that lovely snapping sound when you break it. All the chocolate you buy is already tempered, but if it melts it will go 'out of temper', meaning that its structure is less stable. If you want to work with it and reshape it for use on chocolates or patisserie you need to temper it again before using it for your own creations.

You temper chocolate by taking it through a series of precise temperatures, which are slightly different for white, milk and dark chocolate.

There are many methods of tempering and this book uses the most common. Experienced chocolatiers are able to temper by hand manipulating the chocolate on cold marble slabs, and most professional

chocolatiers have tempering machines that keep a steady supply of tempered chocolate ready for use. In a domestic kitchen the easiest method is the seed method, whereby you introduce some already tempered chocolate (the seed) into some melted chocolate to re-establish the correct structure. A good digital thermometer with a long probe is essential for successful tempering.

How to temper chocolate using the seed method

Make sure you have all your equipment ready, with your chocolate cut into small pieces, your thermometer close by, a knife or palette knife to test if the chocolate is tempered and a heatproof mat so that you can remove the chocolate from the heat rapidly when needed.

1. Place 70 per cent of your chocolate into a heatproof bowl set over a pan of gently simmering water, making sure that the bottom of the bowl does not come into contact with the water below.

2. Allow the chocolate to melt, keeping an eye on the temperature with your thermometer.

3. When it reaches 45–50°C (113–122°F) for dark and milk chocolate, or 40–45°C (104–113°F) for white chocolate, take it off the heat. Try not to allow the chocolate to reach a higher heat.

4. Off the heat add the remaining 30 per cent of chocolate – the seed – and begin to stir the chocolate (*see photo, left*).

5. Keep stirring the chocolate and checking its temperature as it cools. The chocolate now needs to come down to 28–29°C (82.4–84.2°F) for dark chocolate and 27°C (80.6°F) for milk and white chocolate.

6. When the chocolate has reached its

low temperature place it back over the simmering water briefly to bring it up to its working temperature. The working temperature is 32°C (89°F) for dark chocolate and 30°C (86°F) for milk and white chocolate. Do not allow the chocolate to go any higher, or it may well come back out of temper. Work very quickly here to remove the chocolate from the heat at its working temperature, or even before. When working with small quantities of chocolate, the chocolate can rise in temperature very quickly and continue to rise.

7. When you have chocolate at its working temperature, dip a palette knife into the molten chocolate, scrape off one side on the edge of the bowl, and allow the remaining chocolate on the knife to set on your work surface or in the fridge. This is to test if the chocolate is correctly tempered.

8. Touch the set chocolate very lightly indeed (all chocolate will melt with the heat of your finger if you push it firmly). If it feels smooth and dry and doesn't take the impression of your fingertip then it is tempered (*see photo, right*).

9. You now have tempered chocolate to work with. Work quickly while the chocolate remains at a workable consistency. You can warm it lightly with a hairdryer to keep it molten and at working temperature, but be careful not to overheat it and take it out of temper.

Learn with: Fresh Mint Ganache Truffles in Dark Chocolate (page 118) and A Walk in the Black Forest (page 174)

How to temper chocolate in the microwave

The principles and the steps to temper chocolate in a microwave are the same as tempering over a bain-marie. So follow the

instructions above, but using the microwave to melt and heat the chocolate. Use the lowest setting and only apply very short bursts of heat, as the microwave can heat things very quickly, and may well ruin all your hard work if you aren't careful.

ENROBING WITH CHOCOLATE

To enrobe means to coat the filling of a chocolate in tempered chocolate. This will harden and form the shell of the truffle or bonbon.

How to enrobe

Have your ganache or other filling ready to enrobe, as when you have a bowl of tempered chocolate you need to work quickly. The longer you take the thicker the chocolate will become as it cools.

1. Using a large fork (or special enrobing fork with only two prongs), dip each truffle into the molten chocolate to cover.

2. Lift the truffle out, allow the excess chocolate to drip off (*see photo, left*). Place the chocolate on baking paper to set.

3. If you have round ganache balls and you want to use your hands, you can roll the truffles between your hands with some of the tempered chocolate to coat them. This will be messy but you can wear fine disposable gloves. Allow the chocolate coating to set completely before transferring the chocolates to a box or plate.

Learn with: Fresh Mint Ganache Truffles in Dark Chocolate (page 118) and Box of Chocolates (page 160)

EXPERT ADVICE FROM START TO FINISH

This section includes step-by-step advice on some baking skills that you will be using in lots of the recipes. Read them ahead of time so you can start baking with confidence, or refer back to them anytime to refresh your memory.

HOW TO LINE CAKE TINS

Many recipes will need you to prepare your tin, which usually involves greasing it (usually with butter) and lining it in some way. This stops your bake sticking to the tin. Prepare your tin before you start so that your mixture doesn't have to sit and wait.

When you're getting ready to bake, always make sure your tin is clean and dry.

Shallow tins like round sandwich tins or traybake tins should be greased and base-lined. Lightly brush melted butter inside the base, sides and rim (the butter makes a better barrier than oil and tastes nicer than lard or vegetable fat). Set the tin on a sheet of baking paper and draw around it, then cut out the shape and press it onto the base, taking care that there are no creases (*see photo, right*). It is possible to buy ready cut discs to fit most sizes of round cake tin.

Loaf tins should first be lightly brushed inside with melted butter. Then cut a long strip of baking paper that is the same width as the tin base and twice its length (the extra paper each end will help you lift the baked loaf from the tin to save damaging it). Press the paper onto the base and up the short sides to line it (*see photo, right*) – the long sides will not be covered by paper but they are well-greased and once you loosen the cake after baking it will lift out easily. You can also buy loaf tin liners.

HOW TO BUTTER AND FLOUR TINS

Sometimes a recipe will ask you to butter and flour your mould or cake tin. Start by brushing melted butter all over it, as above. Then tip a spoonful or two of plain flour into the tin. Rotating and tapping the tin, coat the interior fully in a fine layer of flour as it sticks to the butter (*see photo, left*). To ensure that it is a fine layer tap the tin sharply a few times on your work surface to knock off any excess. When you have finished tip any loose flour away, or into your next mould if you are filling a series, as you will when you make Chocolate Fondants (see page 86).

HOW TO MAKE PASTRY AND COOKIE DOUGH

Many of the recipes in this book use short doughs. Those for making most tarts or cookies fall into this category. The methods for making, handling and shaping the doughs have much in common, and can benefit from some detailed explanation. Short pastries and doughs need to be handled as little as possible to avoid developing the gluten in the flour. Gluten with a strong structure – with long strands of gluten – is important in bread-making but can make pastry and cookie doughs tough. The fats in pastry also keep it lovely and crumbly: in the oven, they create little pockets of steam giving it a light texture. Try to keep everything as cool as possible as you work.

1. Rub the butter (usually chilled and diced) into the dry ingredients as swiftly as you can until the mixture resembles breadcrumbs. Rubbing in aerates the mixture which will give a lighter texture to your bake. A food-processor is ideal for this, as the cool metal blades can be effective very quickly, and they don't

overheat the dough. You can also rub in using your fingertips, picking up a little of the butter and flour mixture with your fingertips, sliding your thumbs across your fingertips to break down the butter into smaller pieces and letting it fall back into the bowl. To avoid the heat from your hands melting the butter (and cocoa powder if you are using it), you could use two metal round-bladed knives in a crossing action to 'cut in' the butter; work with as few firm strokes as possible. If you shake the bowl, any larger pieces will come to the surface.

2. Add just enough liquid (usually egg, water or milk), working it in gently with a round-bladed knife, until you feel that the dough would come together if pressed. You don't want to add too much or your dough will be tough. The dough should feel soft and sticky. Don't knead the mixture at all, as this could risk developing the gluten.

3. Tip the clumps and crumbs of mixture onto a floured surface and bring them together into a flat disc with floured hands, handling the dough as little as possible (*see photo, right*). Rest the dough before using it, to make it easier to work with and reduce shrinkage later, by wrapping it in clingfilm and chilling it in the fridge for the time indicated in the recipe.

....

Chocolate pastry can be made by adding cocoa powder to a sweet pastry dough. However, it can make it a bit drier, but this is usually solved by adding more liquid or reducing the amount of flour, so do make sure you follow the recipe correctly for successful chocolate pastry (see Baked Chocolate Tarts in Chocolate Pastry, page 134).

HOW TO ROLL DOUGH AND PASTRY

When rolling dough keep your surface lightly floured. You don't want to use too much flour as it could dry out your dough, but you want to keep it from sticking. You will also need to flour your rolling pin, and any cutters if you are making cookies. Keep the rolling pin moving away from you, and move the dough, partially rotating it, each time you roll out. This will prevent the dough from sticking, and ensure it is rolled evenly. When the dough is evenly rolled out to the required thickness you are ready to line your tart tin or cut out your cookies. To avoid getting floury marks on chocolate pastry, you could roll it out between sheets of baking paper instead.

HOW TO CUT OUT COOKIES

Have your prepared baking sheets nearby, so you can drop the cut-out cookies quickly onto them. Using a floured cutter, press down into the dough and bring the cutter back up. Aim to create as clean a line as possible. If the cookie stays on the work surface, lift it gently with a palette knife or spatula. If it comes away in the cutter, lift the cutter over your baking sheet, holding your hand under it to prevent it falling en route, then allow the cookie to fall onto the sheet or ease it out lightly from above with your fingers.

HOW TO LINE A TART TIN WITH PASTRY

Have your tart tin nearby, so you don't have far to lift your delicate pastry. You can test the size of your pastry in relation to your tart case by lifting the tin over the rolled out dough. It is big enough when it is sufficiently bigger than its base to allow for enough pastry to come up the sides.

1. When the pastry is the correct size and thickness, wrap it lightly round the rolling pin, so that it drapes either side. Lift it over to the tart tin and roll the rolling pin away from you, lowering the pastry loosely into the tart case (*see photo 1, page 36*).

2. Working quickly, before the sharp edges of the tart case cut through the delicate pastry, lift a small section of the pastry and lower it back down into the tart tin, easing the dough into the corners as you drop it in and making sure there are no air pockets (*see photo 2, right*). Don't pull or mould the dough, as handling will make it tougher and more liable to shrinkage. If you have any holes or gaps you can fill them with off-cuts.

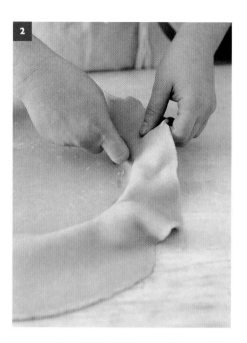

3. The easiest way to trim the top of the tart case is to roll your rolling pin over the surface of the lined tart tin – the sharp edges of the tin will cut off the overhanging pastry (*see photo 3, right*). You can also use a knife. You will need to rest your raw lined tart case in the fridge or freezer again before baking, according to the recipe instructions. In some recipes you can leave the case untrimmed, and cut off the excess pastry after it has baked with a small, serrated knife in a sawing action. The benefit of trimming after you have baked your tart is that it is the only way to be sure you do not have any shrinkage and you can also get a very neat cheffy finish.

HOW TO BLIND BAKE

This is when the pastry case is baked first, without any filling, to ensure that it will be cooked through in your final bake and it won't have a soggy bottom. If you don't bake it blind, the moisture of the filling may prevent it from getting crisp or even cooked.

1. After lining your tin, prick the pastry base using a fork (don't push all the way through or your filling will leak) and chill the pastry in its tin.

2. Lay a piece of baking paper on top of your uncooked pastry, ensuring it covers the base and sides. If you crumple the paper up slightly first it will be easier to fit in.

3. Tip in some baking beans to form a thickish layer to prevent the dough from puffing up as it cooks.

4. Place it in the preheated oven and bake for the time specified in the recipe (usually 15–25 minutes). The length of time you cook it for will depend on whether the tart case will be baked again with a filling, as in the Baked Chocolate Tarts in Chocolate Pastry (see page 134), or whether the blind bake will be its only bake and it needs to be fully cooked, as in the Dark Chocolate Ganache Tart (see page 92).

5. Remove the baking paper and beans for the final 5 minutes of the blind bake to allow the base of the tart to dry out. It can be more difficult to tell when chocolate pastry is done due to the darker colour but it is sufficiently cooked when no damp patches are visible and the base feels sandy.

HOW TO REMOVE A TART FROM ITS TIN

Allow it to cool a little first as this can help prevent the tart from breaking. Cooling will allow the pastry and filling to firm up.

If the sides of the tin are straight rather than fluted, you can slide a small palette knife between the tart and the side of the tin to make sure it releases easily.

For a loose-bottomed tin, sit the base of the tin on an upturned small bowl, glass or can and let the outer ring of the tin fall down around it. You can then remove the base by sliding a wide spatula or palette knife (or two if that gives more support) underneath the tart, then sliding or lifting it onto a flat serving plate, or cooling rack.

HOW TO REMOVE A CAKE FROM ITS TIN

Carefully run a round-bladed knife around the inside of the tin to loosen the cake, and leave it to firm up for 30–60 seconds. To avoid your wire rack leaving marks on the top of a delicate sponge, cover a clean board with a clean, dry tea towel and turn the sponge out upside down onto it. Peel off the lining paper from the base, then set the wire rack on top and turn the whole thing over again. Carefully remove the board and towel. You can then leave the sponge to cool, right side up, on the wire rack.

For very moist cakes that you are going to serve cold, it will be easier to take them out of the tins once they have fully cooled and set. For example brownies can be very hard to handle when hot but are easy when cold.

For fragile cakes that you have baked in a loose-bottomed or springclip tin, it is often best to carefully remove the sides and serve the cake from the base. For example cheesecakes or Chocolate Truffle Cake (see page 74), are very hard to take off their bases. Just place the cake base onto your serving dish.

HOW TO LIFT COOKIES FROM THE BAKING SHEET

Some small bakes are easy to lift from the baking sheet, coming away with no assistance. But there are other cookies or pastries that need more help. This is usually to do with a caramelised mixture that is stickier due to the sugar content. Most thin flat bakes, like the cookies in Chocolate Ice Cream Sandwiches (page 114), are fragile when they first come out of the oven. If you handle them immediately they will become misshapen. But if you leave them too long on the baking trays they stick hard. The secret is to handle them as soon as you feel you can do so and then work quickly. Slide a wide, flat metal spatula underneath each cookie and transfer it quickly, sliding it off carefully onto a wire rack. The cookie can firm up fully as it cools. With very sticky mixture, liked Florentines, it helps to use a lightly oiled or greased spatula, and clean off any sticky bits in between each cookie you lift.

HOW TO FOLD IN

This is the way to delicately combine two or more ingredients – for example adding sifted flour to a creamed cake mixture or incorporating beaten egg whites – so that you don't knock out all the air you've carefully beaten or whisked in.

Use the edge of a large spoon or plastic spatula to cut down cleanly through the centre of the mixture until you touch the bottom of the bowl, then turn the spoon right-way up and bring it up through the mixture to the top (*see photo, right*). Turn the spoon over so that the contents flop gently onto the rest of the mixture. Give the bowl a quarter turn so that you start from a different place, then cut down again through the mixture, lift it and flop it over. Keep doing this folding action, using the least number of movements, until you can't see any more unmixed streaks.

HOW TO WHISK EGG WHITES

Whisking incorporates air into a mixture to provide volume and structure and is essential for meringues, macarons and

soufflés. Whether you're whisking whole eggs or just their whites, eggs should always be at room temperature. This helps them expand to their maximum volume. You need a large, spotlessly clean and grease-free bowl (any trace of fat or yolk stuck to the bowl or whisk will prevent the whites from being beaten successfully – run the cut side of a lemon half around the inside of the bowl and over the whisk to be really sure).

Put the egg whites in the bowl and whisk on a low speed (or slowly by hand) for about 30 seconds so they become frothy and the structure starts to develop. If you add a pinch of cream of tartar or a drop of lemon juice at this point the slight acidity will help the structure to stiffen, which helps achieve maximum volume. Increase the speed and continue whisking until the mixture is a mass of tiny bubbles with a very smooth and fine texture. To tell if the whites have reached soft peak stage, lift the whisk out – you should get a peak of egg whites that slightly droops down (*see photo, above left*).

After a little more whisking, the next stage is stiff peak, when the peak should stand upright with no droop (*see photo, below left*). You should also be able to turn the bowl upside down and hold it over your head (or the work surface, if you're not feeling quite so adventurous) without the whites falling out.

ROASTING NUTS

Nuts are one of the most frequent ingredient partners for chocolate. In many recipes nuts benefit from roasting before using, as it brings out and intensifies their flavours. It is easiest to roast nuts on the hob, as you can see them as they colour and have more control over the process. Place your nuts into a wide, flat frying pan, so that they are no more than one nut deep, over a medium heat. Shake the nuts to turn them over as they heat up. Watch them carefully, as the oils in nuts can catch and burn quickly. When the nuts have turned golden and you can smell them toasting, remove them from the heat and allow to cool before using.

PRALINE

Praline, or caramelised nuts, is used in many chocolates and chocolate recipes. Nuts are combined with caramelised sugar and then used whole, chopped or ground. It is delicious to eat in its own right, and is a perfect partner for chocolate as in the Chocolate and Praline Roulade or the Hazelnut Dacquoise with Dark Chocolate and Praline (see page 130 or 148).

How to make praline

1. Put a baking sheet or tin near the stove ready to pour the praline onto when cooked.
2. Then place the nuts, water and sugar in a small pan over a high heat until they are boiling, stirring continuously with a wooden or heatproof spatula, so they do not catch on the bottom of the pan and burn.
3. Then continue to stir as the water boils off and the mixture becomes dry and sandy.
4. Keep stirring, being careful not to let any one part of the contents of the pan catch, as the sugar then melts, turns golden brown, and coats the nuts.
5. As soon as all the sugar has caramelised and you have a nice even colour, take the pan off the heat and pour the nuts onto your waiting cold baking sheet (*see photo, right*).
6. Leave the praline aside to cool. At no point touch the mixture as molten sugar reaches dangerously high temperatures.
7. When the praline is cold it can be broken up, chopped or ground for use.

MAKING CUSTARD

Custard is at the base of, or accompanies, many favourite recipes. The ice cream recipes in this book are custard based, and the crème pâtissière involved in so many bakes (such as the éclairs on page 110) follows the same principles too. Mastering custard will allow you to tackle many different recipes. Before you start ensure that you have all your equipment and ingredients to hand. You don't want to be dashing to find a spoon to stir with, or a whisk to beat with, when the mixture is over the heat. It is constant stirring and movement that will allow the eggs and milk or cream to cook together smoothly and not curdle.

1. Heat your milk or cream to just below boiling point. While it is heating whisk the egg yolks and any sugar in a bowl just alongside your stove.

2. When the cream is hot, pour it over the eggs, whisking continuously as you do so, and then pour the whisked mixture back into the pan. Cook the custard mixture over a low-medium heat, stirring continuously, until it has thickened sufficiently for your recipe (*see photo, left*). This can take up to 15–20 minutes if you have the heat very low.

3. Leave your custard or crème pâtissière to cool with a piece of clingfilm covering its surface to prevent a skin forming.

PIPING WITH CHOCOLATE

Piped chocolate can be a striking and easy way to decorate your bakes. As melted chocolate is liquid it flows readily from the finest piping hole, to allow you to create fine lines, dots, lettering and other patterns.

How to fill a piping bag

1. Drop the piping nozzle, if you are using one, into the piping bag, then snip off just

enough of the tip so that the nozzle fits snugly.

2. Twist the bag right above the nozzle or secure it with a wide clip (so the mixture doesn't ooze out while you're filling it), then put the bag in a tall glass or jug and fold the top of the bag over the rim (the container will support the bag so that it's easier to fill).

3. Spoon the mixture into the bag until about two-thirds full (*see photo, right*).

4. Unfold the bag from the rim and twist the top to push the mixture down to the (still twisted) nozzle end, pushing out any air pockets, then twist it again to compact the mixture and prevent it escaping.

5. Untwist the nozzle end and squeeze the bag so that the mixture fills the nozzle. Practise the flow and shape of the piping before you begin.

How to pipe

When piping use one hand at the base of the piping bag, on the nozzle if you are using one, to steady your piping. Use the other hand to hold the top of the bag, keeping the mixture inside the twisted top, and squeezing to push mixture through the tip. You will need to stop periodically as the piping bag empties, to twist the top of the bag again and ensure the mixture is tightly packed down on the tip. Hold the bag vertically upright when piping. This allows much greater control. Because chocolate hardens as it cools, particularly as it thins out, you may need to remove hardened chocolate from the tip of a piping bag as you work, to release it. It makes sense to prepare everything you will need to work with before you get the chocolate ready to pipe, and then work quickly before it starts to harden.

Help!

Baking and working with chocolate is a delicious challenge, and of course sometimes things go wrong no matter how careful you have been! Here are some frequently encountered problems, and some expert tips on how to get back on track.

MY GANACHE HAS SPLIT!

If your ganache appears oily, with oil separated on the surface, it has split. Try to avoid this happening by stirring the cream into the chocolate gently and gradually – the process of amalgamation is akin to making mayonnaise. If it has split you can often bring it back to a smooth consistency with an extra spoonful or two of cold cream and then beating vigorously. Conversely a drop or two of boiling water and a vigorous beating can also work.

THERE ARE WHITE MARKS ON MY CHOCOLATE!

If your chocolate is within its sell by date, but has creamy white streaks and is soft to the touch, that means that it has come out of temper. It is still perfectly fine to use in a bake if you are going to melt and incorporate it into a mixture. If you want to use it in whole pieces or for decoration you will need to temper it again.

MY TEMPERING HASN'T WORKED!

Chocolate is sensitive stuff, and the temperatures needed to temper it are precise. It is entirely possible that the temperature of the day, or of your kitchen, or the atmosphere, can make it fail despite your hard work. Be as precise as possible to give yourself the best chance of success. When the chocolate is tempered don't overwork it, or that can cause it to lose its fine structure. If your temper test clearly shows that the chocolate isn't tempered you will have to start again. There are also lots of recipes in this book that don't involve tempering, or in which you could use melted chocolate instead if you know you are going to eat them quickly.

MY CHOCOLATE HAS GONE GRAINY!

Unfortunately, if chocolate gets too hot and scorches, it goes grainy. If this happens you do have to start again, as it can't regain its smoothness. Avoid this by never letting chocolate come into contact with direct heat, and always ensuring that the simmering water in your bain-marie cannot touch the bottom of the bowl.

MY CAKE MIXTURE HAS SPLIT!

Incorporating eggs into a batter can result in something that looks much like scrambled eggs. To avoid this always use room temperature eggs, so the temperature shock is not too great between the egg and the rest of the mixture. To bring the mixture back add a tablespoon of the flour or dry ingredients you have yet to add, and beat the mixture until smooth.

MY CUSTARD LOOKS SEPARATED!

The risk with making custard is that it separates, and becomes scrambled egg in hot cream. To avoid this don't let the mixture get too hot, and always stir continuously as it cooks. If it does start to split plunge the pan into a waiting bowl or sink of cold water, so that the water can come up the sides of your pan to cool it. Then whisk the custard vigorously, preferably with a rotary whisk.

THE TOP OF MY CAKE/PASTRY IS GETTING TOO BROWN!

If the top of your cake or the tips of your pastry are getting too dark, but the middle of your bake isn't cooked yet, cover the top or the darkened crust with tin foil. This should allow the bake to continue cooking without the edges or top getting any darker. It can be more difficult to gauge whether your chocolate bake is over-browning due to the darker colour of the mixture, so keep a careful eye on it.

MY BROWNIES ARE UNDERDONE!

With a moist bake like brownies, where you want the inside to be fudgy and soft, you want to avoid overcooking it so you don't end up with dry cake. But if you find out later that you have taken them out too soon, and the inside is underdone, put the brownies in the fridge to set further. You can cut and serve them from the fridge and they will be firm and still taste delicious. You will learn what the exact correct time is for a given recipe in your oven.

MY PASTRY IS TOUGH!

The secret to tender, crumbly, buttery pastry is not to overwork it. Try to handle it as little as possible. Bring it together into a flat disc as soon as it forms a dough. When it comes to rolling it out, flour the surfaces very lightly, so that you don't dry out the dough with too much additional flour. Keep the dough moving as you roll it too, so that it doesn't stick to your surface, and try to avoid rerolling. Any extra handling will just make it tougher. There's not much you can do once it has been rolled out and cooked, but you'll get more proficient with practice, and in the meantime all homemade dough tastes wonderful! So don't worry too much.

BAKE IT BETTER

Recipes

Cocoa Stars

This is the simplest of chocolate cookies, but no less delicious for it. Cocoa powder flavours a simple dough that can be cut into shapes or simply shaped by hand.

200g unsalted butter, softened
215g caster sugar
290g plain flour
1 teaspoon baking powder
2 teaspoons vanilla extract
1 medium egg, at room temperature
4 tablespoons cocoa powder

HANDS-ON TIME:
25 minutes

BAKING TIME:
10–12 minutes

MAKES:
34 cookies

SPECIAL EQUIPMENT:
2 baking sheets,
6cm star cutter

STORAGE:
Keep for up to
5 days in an airtight container

1. Preheat the oven to 200°C (180°C fan), 400°F, Gas 6. Line the baking sheet with baking paper.

2. Place all the ingredients into a large bowl and mix, first with a wooden spoon and then with your hands, until you can bring it together into a soft dough.

3. Lightly flour a work surface and your rolling pin and **roll** the dough out to a thickness of roughly 1cm. Using a 6cm star cookie cutter, **cut** shapes out of the dough and place them on the prepared baking sheets, leaving a little space between each cookie, as they will spread slightly during cooking. Gather the dough off-cuts into a ball and re-roll to make more shapes.

4. Bake the cookies in the oven for 10 minutes, before checking to see whether their tops are all crackled. If they still look raw and damp, rather than crackled, return them to the oven for a couple more minutes.

5. The cookies will be very soft, so leave them to cool on the baking sheets for 10 minutes until firmed up a little, before you **lift** them onto a wire rack to cool completely.

Try Something Different

To decorate these cookies with piped white chocolate, **melt** 50g white chocolate and put it into a small disposable piping bag. Snip off the tip and pipe stripes or zigzags over the cookies and leave to set.

You could also sandwich two cookies together with a simple buttercream: mash together 100g softened butter with 200g icing sugar, a teaspoon of water and a few drops of vanilla extract until smooth.

If you don't want to use cookie cutters roll teaspoons of the dough into walnut-sized balls with your hands. Flatten them slightly on the baking sheets before baking. Then they will form round, domed cookies.

Dark Chocolate and Walnut Muffins

Muffins are one of the easiest bakes to make at home. You simply stir the wet ingredients into the dry. These contain the wonderful combination of dark chocolate and walnuts.

285ml buttermilk
2 medium eggs, at room temperature
1 teaspoon vanilla extract
150g unsalted butter, melted
150g plain flour
150g wholemeal flour
2 teaspoons baking powder

1 teaspoon bicarbonate of soda
pinch of salt
185g caster sugar
100g 70 per cent dark chocolate chips or chunks
100g walnuts, roughly chopped

1. Preheat the oven to 190°C (170°C fan), 375°F, Gas 5 and fill a 12-hole muffin tin with large muffin cases.

2. Put the buttermilk, eggs, vanilla and melted butter into a large jug and whisk them together. Next sift both flours, the baking powder, bicarbonate of soda and a pinch of salt into a large mixing bowl. Stir in the sugar and make a well in the centre of the dry ingredients.

3. Pour the buttermilk mixture into the well and stir the wet ingredients into the dry with a large spatula until they are only just combined. The secret to good muffins is not to overmix. The mixture will remain lumpy looking, but that doesn't matter – just make sure you don't have any pockets of unincorporated flour.

4. Add the chocolate chips or chunks and walnuts and **fold** them in with just a couple of strokes. Spoon the muffin mixture into the tin, dividing it evenly between the muffin cases. Bake the muffins for 20 minutes until they are puffed up and golden. Let them cool in the tin for about 5 minutes and then transfer to a wire rack to finish cooling.

Try Something Different

The wholemeal flour gives these muffins a nutty quality, but you can make them with all plain flour. You can also mix and match the chocolate and nuts to suit your taste; try white chocolate and pistachios or milk chocolate and pecans.

Easy does it

HANDS-ON TIME:
15 minutes

BAKING TIME:
20 minutes

MAKES:
12 muffins

SPECIAL EQUIPMENT:
12-hole muffin tin, muffin cases

STORAGE:
Best eaten on the day you make them but they can also be frozen. Once cold, pop the muffins into an airtight freezer bag and freeze for up to 3 months

Simple Chocolate Truffles

These simple truffles are impressive, delicious, and very simple to make, just combining cream and chocolate into a **ganache**. This is a chance to make your own chocolates out of your favourite chocolate!

300g 70 per cent dark chocolate (try Virunga, Vietnam or other complex origins)
300ml double cream
50g butter, cut into small pieces
cocoa powder, for dusting

1. Ensure the chocolate is broken into small pieces, so that it has the best chance to melt evenly, and put it into a heatproof bowl. Next put the cream in a small pan and place over a medium heat until it just comes up to the boil. Remove from the heat and let it sit for a minute to cool a little.

2. Pour the hot cream over the chocolate and stir to melt, gradually incorporating all the chocolate into the cream to make a **ganache**. Then add the butter, piece by piece, and beat the ganache until it is all smoothly amalgamated.

3. Pour the ganache into a square cake tin lined with clingfilm, or leave in its bowl if you want to hand roll the truffles later. Place in the fridge to chill for at least 1 hour, so it is firm enough to form into truffles.

4. When you are ready to form the truffles, prepare a wide, shallow bowl covered with cocoa powder. Either **cut the ganache** into cubes with a warmed knife, or scoop out small spoonfuls and **roll the ganache** into balls between cocoa-dusted hands. Toss the cubes or balls into the cocoa powder and turn them to dust on all sides.

5. Store the finished truffles in the fridge in an airtight container until a little before you wish to serve them. You don't want to serve them quite fridge cold, but they will soften quickly in a warm room (about 10 minutes out of the fridge will be long enough). They also freeze very well, and take very little time to defrost (about 2 hours).

Try Something Different

You can roll the shaped truffles in a variety of things instead of cocoa powder, to change the flavour and texture. Try icing sugar, finely chopped nuts such as pistachios, crushed freeze-dried raspberries or crushed honeycomb.

Easy does it

HANDS-ON TIME:
45 minutes

HANDS-OFF TIME:
1 hour chilling

MAKES:
25–40 truffles, depending on size

SPECIAL EQUIPMENT:
Square cake tin (optional)

METHOD USED:
Chocolate ganache, page 26

STORAGE:
Keep in an airtight container in the fridge for up to 10 days

Hot Chocolate Cupcakes with Vanilla Icing

These simple cakes take their name from the hot chocolate powder used to make them. This is one of the easiest and most reliable chocolate cake recipes there is.

HANDS-ON TIME:
25 minutes

BAKING TIME:
20 minutes

MAKES:
12 large cupcakes

SPECIAL
EQUIPMENT:
12-hole muffin tin,
muffin cases

STORAGE:
Keep for up to
5 days in an airtight
container

For the cupcakes

150g unsalted butter, softened
150g caster sugar
5 medium eggs, at room temperature
200g hot/drinking chocolate powder
2 tablespoons milk
100g plain flour
pinch of salt

For the vanilla icing

125g unsalted butter, softened
250g icing sugar
1 teaspoon vanilla extract, or to taste
1 tablespoon warm water, if necessary

1. Preheat the oven to 180°C (160°C fan), 350°F, Gas 4 and fill a 12-hole muffin tin with large muffin cases.

2. In a large mixing bowl cream the butter and sugar together until light and fluffy. Add the eggs one by one, alternating with the chocolate powder, beating the mixture after each addition until it is smooth. Lastly **fold** in the milk, flour and salt.

3. Spoon an equal amount of the mixture into each of the 12 cases in your muffin tin. Bake in the oven for 20 minutes, or until they are risen, with cracked tops, and a skewer comes out with only a little wet crumb attached. You don't want to overcook the cakes as they will continue to cook a little after they come out of the oven and are nicest a little fudgy.

4. Leave the cakes on a wire rack to cool while you prepare the icing. Put the butter into a medium-sized bowl and add a few large spoonfuls of the icing sugar. Using a fork, mash the sugar into the butter to create a smooth, lump-free icing. It is easiest to do this by adding a little of the sugar at a time, as small amounts will dissolve into the butter easily; if you add a lot of sugar at once it can be very dry and hard to work with. When you have some of the sugar added you can add the vanilla, and if you feel the icing is dry add some or all of the water. You want a thick spreadable icing, so add the liquid cautiously, as it is easy to make the icing too runny.

5. Top each cooled cupcake with a heaped teaspoonful of icing and spread it to cover with a knife or palette knife.

Try Something Different

You can ice these with coffee or chocolate fudge icing – you will need double the amount given for the Coffee Bourbons (see page 60). Top with anything decorative, such as sweets, chocolate buttons or edible flowers.

Pecan and Milk Chocolate Chip Cookies

Chocolate chip cookies are always a crowd-pleaser. This dough is easy to put together and is frozen until you need the cookies – you just slice and bake straight from the freezer. The sweetness of pecans marries well with the fudgy taste of milk chocolate.

120g unsalted butter, at room temperature
150g caster sugar
1 medium egg, at room temperature
½ teaspoon vanilla extract
200g plain flour

generous pinch of salt
¼ teaspoon baking powder
75g 35 per cent minimum milk chocolate chips or chunks
75g pecan nuts

1. Put the butter and sugar into a large bowl and cream them together with a wooden spoon until fully blended and light and fluffy. Next beat in the egg and vanilla extract. Add the flour, salt and baking powder to the bowl and beat it into the butter mixture to form a soft dough. Then stir in the chocolate and nuts.

2. Turn the dough out onto a lightly floured surface, flour your hands and ease and roll the dough into a log shape roughly 40cm long by 5cm wide. Then lift the log carefully onto a large piece of clingfilm. Wrap the dough in the clingfilm and place it in the freezer to harden for at least 4 hours. (The dough will be soft and not that easy to handle, so just go lightly, with well-floured hands.)

3. When you are ready to bake the cookies, preheat the oven to 180°C (160°C fan), 350°F, Gas 4 and line two baking sheets with baking paper.

4. Remove the frozen cookie log from the freezer and unwrap. Using a sharp knife, slice the log into 16 equal slices. Place the cookie slices spaced well apart on the baking sheets and bake in the oven for 12–15 minutes, taking them out when they are golden at the edges and no raw mixture is visible. You don't want to over-bake them, as a chewy centre is the ideal for a classic chocolate chip cookie. **Lift** them onto a wire rack to cool.

Try Something Different

You can use any combination of nuts and chocolate for these cookies; dark chocolate and almond is delicious, as is white chocolate with pistachio. If you don't like nuts just leave them out and use double the amount of chocolate!
You can easily double the quantities of this recipe to make two dough logs; keep one to bake another day.

HANDS-ON TIME:
15 minutes

HANDS-OFF TIME:
About 4 hours freezing, or until you need them

BAKING TIME:
12–15 minutes

MAKES:
16 cookies

SPECIAL EQUIPMENT:
2 baking sheets

STORAGE:
Keep the unbaked dough log in the freezer for up to 3 months; baked cookies keep for up to 1 week in an airtight container

A fast and easy no-yeast, no-knead bread. Here the delicious taste and texture of cocoa nibs works really well with the nuttiness of the oats and wholemeal flour. Wonderful spread with cream cheese or goat's cheese.

300g white spelt flour
200g plain wholemeal flour
150g oats
100g cocoa nibs
1 tablespoon bicarbonate of soda
1 teaspoon salt
568ml buttermilk
3 tablespoons runny honey

Easy does it

HANDS-ON TIME:
15 minutes

BAKING TIME:
35 minutes

MAKES:
1 round loaf

SPECIAL
EQUIPMENT:
Baking sheet

STORAGE:
Best eaten on the
day you bake it

1. Preheat the oven to 200°C (180°C fan), 400°F, Gas 6 and lightly dust a baking sheet with flour.

2. Put all the dry ingredients into a large bowl, stir them to combine, and then make a well in the centre.

3. Pour the buttermilk into the well. Add the honey to the buttermilk and mix it into the buttermilk to make it easier to stir it into the flour. Then work the dry ingredients into the wet ingredients to make a loose dough.

4. Flour your hands before turning the soda bread dough out onto a lightly floured surface. Shape the dough into a ball and flatten the top slightly – don't be tempted to knead the dough as overworking will make it tough. Place this ball onto the flour-dusted baking sheet. Then take a sharp, serrated knife and score a deep cross in the surface of the dough before dusting the loaf with flour.

5. Place the baking sheet on the middle shelf of the oven and bake the loaf for 35 minutes. When you take it out and tap the bottom of the loaf it should make a hollow sound. (If it doesn't, return it to the oven for another 5 minutes.)

6. Place the cooked loaf on a wire rack to cool and cover it completely with a damp tea towel until you are ready to eat it. This helps to keep the soda bread from drying out as it cools.

Try Something Different

If you keep to the basic quantities of this recipe you can vary the type of flour. It is very nice with all white flour or all spelt flour.
Nuts work well in this bread, as well as or instead of the cocoa nibs. Add 100g of walnuts just before forming the dough into a ball.

Coffee Bourbons

A coffee-infused alternative to the traditional chocolate bourbon biscuit, crisp cocoa-rich biscuits sandwiched together with a coffee fudge icing. Perfect alongside a cup of coffee.

HANDS-ON TIME:
40 minutes

HANDS-OFF TIME:
30 minutes chilling

BAKING TIME:
10 minutes

MAKES:
26 sandwich biscuits

SPECIAL
EQUIPMENT:
2 baking sheets,
rectangular cookie
cutter (optional)

STORAGE:
Keep for up to
1 week in an airtight
container

For the biscuits

125g unsalted butter
125g caster sugar
1 tablespoon golden syrup
1 medium egg, at room temperature
225g plain flour
pinch of salt
½ teaspoon bicarbonate of soda
40g cocoa powder
1–2 tablespoons milk

For the coffee fudge icing

175g icing sugar
2 teaspoons instant coffee granules
60g unsalted butter
60g caster sugar
2 tablespoons water

1. To make the biscuits, cream the butter and sugar together in a mixing bowl until light and fluffy. Add the syrup and egg, and beat everything together to combine. Next add the flour, salt, bicarbonate of soda and cocoa powder and gradually work them into the butter mixture with a wooden spoon until combined. Drizzle in as much milk as you need to just bring the ingredients together into a stiff dough. Pat into a flattened ball using lightly floured hands, then wrap the dough in clingfilm and chill in the fridge for 30 minutes.

2. Preheat the oven to 180°C (160°C fan), 350°F, Gas 4 and line two baking sheets with baking paper.

3. Take the dough out of the fridge and **roll** it out on a lightly floured surface to the thickness of a £1 coin. **Cut** even-sized rectangles with a knife or cutter and place them on your prepared baking sheets. (You can of course use any shaped cutter you like.) Bake the biscuits for 10 minutes, and then **lift** them onto a wire rack to cool.

4. To make the coffee fudge icing, sift the icing sugar into a bowl and add the coffee granules. Then put the butter, caster sugar and water into a small pan and melt over a medium heat, stirring occasionally. When the ingredients have fully melted, turn up the heat and bring to the boil. Pour the bubbling liquid over the icing sugar and coffee, beating it well with a wooden spoon to mix everything together and get rid of any lumps or undissolved coffee. Leave the icing to cool a little, during which time it will thicken up to a spreadable consistency.

5. When both the biscuits and icing have cooled, spread a little icing on one side of half the biscuits and sandwich together with the other biscuits.

Try Something Different

For a more traditional Bourbon biscuit, replace the coffee in the icing recipe with 2 tablespoons of cocoa powder to make a chocolate fudge icing.

Pistachio and Dark Chocolate Financiers

Financiers, so called because they became popular in the financial district of Paris in the 1890s, are easy to mix together. Nuts and chocolate are perfect partners, and here crisp, almost savoury, pistachios contrast with the chocolate melted within the financiers.

80g unsalted butter
50g pistachios (shelled and unsalted)
35g ground almonds
75g icing sugar
20g plain flour

2 medium egg whites, at room temperature
½ teaspoon vanilla extract
18 65 per cent dark chocolate chunks or buttons (about 30g)

1. Preheat the oven to 170°C (150°C fan), 325°F, Gas 3. Put a 9-hole silicone mini cake mould onto a baking sheet for support, or, if you are using a metal cake tin, **butter** it well.

2. First put the butter in a small pan and melt it over a medium heat to make a beurre noisette. This means leaving it after melting until it deepens in colour to pale brown, loses its milky smell and smells lightly nutty. Once you have reached this stage leave the butter to cool a little.

3. Put 30g of the pistachios into a food-processor and whizz until finely ground (you are looking for a powdery consistency). Chop the remaining 20g pistachios and put to one side.

4. Mix together the ground pistachios, ground almonds, icing sugar and flour. It is best to do this in a large jug, as the finished mixture is very wet and this will make it easy to pour into the moulds. Add the melted butter and then the egg whites and mix until everything is fully incorporated.

5. Pour the mixture into the moulds, making sure each mould is no more than two-thirds full. Push two pieces of chocolate down into each raw financier and top them with the chopped pistachios.

6. Bake in the oven for 15–20 minutes, until they are risen and golden brown. Let the cakes cool in their moulds for a few moments before easing out onto a wire rack to cool.

Try Something Different

These can be made with any combination of ground nuts. Try them with 65g ground almonds in place of the ground almonds and pistachios, then bake with 20g slivered almonds on top.
You can vary the chocolate and chopped nuts, or substitute different toppings. They are delicious with raspberries – push a couple of berries down into the batter before baking.

Easy does it

HANDS-ON TIME:
20 minutes

BAKING TIME:
15–20 minutes

MAKES:
9 financiers

SPECIAL EQUIPMENT:
9-hole mini cake tin or mould

STORAGE:
Keep in an airtight container for up to 5 days

Cocoa Nib and Chocolate Chip Granola Bar

A crunchy treat, made easily by stirring everything together and then baking. The double chocolate hit of cocoa nibs and dark chocolate gives this extra texture and taste. The chocolate topping is, of course, optional.

100g blanched almonds
150g unsalted butter
300g caster sugar
4 tablespoons (70g) golden syrup
350g jumbo oats
50g cocoa nibs
1 teaspoon ground cinnamon

large pinch of salt
100g sunflower seeds
100g 65 per cent dark chocolate chips

For the chocolate topping
150g dark or milk chocolate

Easy does it

HANDS-ON TIME:
15 minutes

BAKING TIME:
20 minutes

MAKES:
18 granola bars

SPECIAL
EQUIPMENT:
23cm square brownie
or cake tin

STORAGE:
Keep for up to
1 week in an airtight
container

1. Preheat the oven to 200°C (180°C fan), 400°F, Gas 6. Grease and **line** the base and sides of the baking tin with baking paper.

2. Put the almonds into a dry frying pan and **roast** them over a low heat until they colour slightly. You should be able to smell them toasting and hear them crackle slightly. Take them off the heat and then set the almonds to one side to cool.

3. Put the butter, sugar and syrup together in a large pan and melt them together over a medium heat until the mixture is just bubbling. Take the pan off the heat before adding the oats, nibs, cinnamon, salt and sunflower seeds. Roughly chop the cooled almonds and add them in too.

4. Stir the contents of the pan thoroughly so that all the oats, nuts and seeds are coated in the sugar mixture. Lastly add in the chocolate chips with a couple of swift strokes – you don't want the chocolate to melt too much in the hot mixture, but to remain in separate pieces in the granola bar.

5. Spoon the mixture into the prepared tin and press it down to create an even, flat surface. Bake the granola in the oven for 20 minutes. When you take it out it should be golden, caramelised and bubbling at the edges. Leave the granola mixture to cool in the tin on a wire rack for about 5 minutes before turning it out and cutting it up into bars.

6. **Melt** the chocolate for the topping in a bain-marie; break the chocolate into pieces so it has the best chance to melt evenly. Dip the top of each granola bar in the molten chocolate then allow to set.

Try Something Different

You can mix up the nuts and chocolate. Macadamia and white chocolate are a delicious combination.

Brownies

This crowd-pleasing chocolate bake is easy to make. The chocolate is simply **melted** and stirred through the other ingredients before baking. The secret of a fudgy brownie is not to overcook it.

200g 70–75 per cent dark chocolate
250g unsalted butter
3 medium eggs, at room temperature
250g caster sugar
200g self-raising flour
large pinch of salt

1. Preheat the oven to 180°C (160°C fan), 350°F, Gas 4. Grease and **line** the base and sides of the baking tin with baking paper.

2. Break the chocolate into pieces and place with the butter in a small pan over a very low heat. Keep an eye on it, stirring occasionally and breaking up the butter into smaller pieces, to **melt** the butter and chocolate together.

3. Break the eggs into a large bowl, add the sugar and **whisk** them together until lighter in colour and mousse-like. Continue whisking the egg and sugar mixture while pouring in the melted chocolate and butter, and keep going until the two are fully mixed together. Now **fold** in the flour and salt until everything is fully combined.

4. Pour the brownie mixture into your prepared tin and bake in the oven for 20 minutes. If you test the brownie with a skewer at this point it will not come out clean, but should have a little moist crumb sticking to it. This is what you are looking for: you don't want lots of raw mixture, but you do want it to have the desirable fudgy centre. The brownie will continue to set and firm up while you leave it to cool in the tin on a wire rack.

5. Once the brownie is fully cold, **remove from the tin** and cut it into squares.

Try Something Different

Walnuts are a classic addition to brownies; simply add 150g roughly chopped walnuts to the finished mixture just before pouring it into the tin to bake. Or for a sweeter treat add a handful of mini marshmallows.

HANDS-ON TIME:
20 minutes

BAKING TIME:
20 minutes

MAKES:
16 brownies

SPECIAL EQUIPMENT:
23cm square brownie or cake tin

METHOD USED:
Melting chocolate, page 24

STORAGE:
Keep in the fridge for up to 1 week

Blueberry Blondies

The white chocolate version of a brownie, they are just as easy to bake. The recipes are similar, but white chocolate is sweeter so less sugar is added to the mixture; it also has a longer bake time due to the higher fat content. The addition of dried blueberries offsets the sweetness of white chocolate.

250g unsalted butter
200g white chocolate, broken into pieces
3 medium eggs, at room temperature
200g caster sugar

200g self-raising flour
large pinch of salt
150g dried blueberries

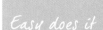
HANDS-ON TIME:
20 minutes

BAKING TIME:
30 minutes

MAKES:
16 blondies

SPECIAL EQUIPMENT:
23cm square brownie or cake tin

METHOD USED:
Melting chocolate, page 24

STORAGE:
Keep in the fridge for up to 1 week

1. Preheat the oven to 180°C (160°C fan), 350°F, Gas 4. Grease and **line** the base and sides of the baking tin with baking paper.

2. Put the butter and chocolate into a small pan and place over a very low heat. Keep an eye on it, stirring occasionally and breaking up the butter into smaller pieces, to **melt** the butter and chocolate together. The white chocolate may stay lumpy as the higher fat content in white chocolate can make it trickier to melt smoothly, but take the pan off the heat and whisk with a small hand whisk to amalgamate the two as far as possible.

3. Break the eggs into a large bowl, add the sugar and **whisk** them together until lighter in colour and mousse-like. Continue whisking the egg and sugar mixture while pouring in the chocolate and butter, and keep going until the two are fully mixed together. Now **fold** in the flour and salt until everything is fully combined. Finally fold in the blueberries.

4. Pour the blondie mixture into your prepared tin and bake for 30 minutes, until just set. If you test the blondie with a skewer at this point it will not come out clean, but should have a little moist crumb sticking to it. This is what you are looking for: you don't want lots of raw mixture, but you do want it to have the desirable fudgy centre. The blondie will continue to set and firm up while you leave it to cool in the tin on a wire rack.

5. Once the blondie is cold, **remove from the tin** and cut into squares.

Try Something Different

Vary the dried fruit you use; anything with enough acidity to contrast with the sweetness of white chocolate will work well (replacing the blueberries with the same amount of chopped prunes is particularly good).
As with brownies, adding nuts is delicious, and for something really decadent add dark chocolate chips. Stir in 100–200g of whatever combination of things you choose just before baking.

Chocolate Loaf Cake

Now that you have mastered several small bakes and tray bakes, it's time to try this rich loaf cake, made with melted dark chocolate and ground almonds. This is a plain cake, so lends itself to any time of day, or can be served as a pudding with ice cream.

150g unsalted butter
150g 70–75 per cent dark chocolate, broken into pieces
150g golden syrup
4 medium eggs, at room temperature
50g caster sugar

125g plain flour
75g ground almonds
1 teaspoon bicarbonate of soda
pinch of salt
3 tablespoons milk

HANDS-ON TIME:
20 minutes

BAKING TIME:
45 minutes

MAKES:
1 loaf cake

SPECIAL EQUIPMENT:
900g loaf tin

METHOD USED:
Melting chocolate, page 24

STORAGE:
Keep for up to 1 week wrapped in foil in an airtight container

1. Preheat the oven to 180°C (160°C fan), 350°F, Gas 4. Grease and **line** the base and sides of your loaf tin with baking paper or a loaf tin liner.

2. Put the butter, chocolate and syrup into a pan and **melt** them together over a low heat, stirring occasionally to mix them together. Remove from the heat and put to one side.

3. Then **whisk** the eggs and sugar with a hand-held rotary whisk for about 5 minutes (or use a hand-held electric whisk), until they are pale and mousse-like. Whisk in your melted butter, chocolate and syrup mixture, just until it is fully incorporated. Then **fold** in the flour, ground almonds, bicarbonate of soda and salt to form a smooth batter. Add the milk and fold that in until it is fully mixed in.

4. Pour your batter (it will be quite liquid) into the lined loaf tin and bake it on the middle shelf of the oven for 45 minutes. The cake is done when a skewer comes out with no liquid mixture attached. This cake has a very moist crumb, so it won't come out completely clean.

5. Place the cake in its tin on a wire rack to cool completely before you **remove from the tin**. To keep the cake at its best, wrap it in foil once cold – it gets more delicious over the next few days.

Try Something Different

To make a white chocolate glaze, melt 100g white chocolate with 25ml double cream in a bain-marie, then spread over the loaf. Allow to set before slicing.

Cinnamon and Chocolate Tiger Bundt Cake

A classic cake with a delicate flavour twist. This is made using a basic sponge cake batter, which is divided to create two flavours that are swirled together to give tiger stripes inside.

250g unsalted butter, softened
250g caster sugar
4 medium eggs, at room temperature
250g self-raising flour

pinch of salt
¾ teaspoon ground cinnamon
1 tablespoon cocoa powder
7 tablespoons milk

1. Preheat the oven to 180°C (160°C fan), 350°F, Gas 4 and liberally **butter** the bundt tin.

2. Cream the butter and sugar together until they are really light and creamy. Then add the eggs one by one with a little of the flour if necessary to prevent the mixture from curdling. Then **fold** in the rest of the flour and the salt.

3. Divide the cake mixture into two by moving half the mixture to a separate bowl. Add the cinnamon and 3 tablespoons of the milk to one bowl and fold the mixture gently until all the milk and cinnamon are stirred in and you have a nice dropping consistency. This means that the mixture will drop from a spoon back into the bowl if you hold a full spoon of batter above the bowl. If the batter is still too stiff then add a little extra milk. Spoon this batter into the bottom of the bundt tin, making a little valley in a ring around the centre and encouraging the mixture about halfway up the sides.

4. Next take the second half of the cake batter and add the cocoa powder and remaining 4 tablespoons of milk. Mix this half of the batter just until everything is smoothly combined. Then spoon the cocoa cake batter evenly on top of the cinnamon batter, into the well you have created.

5. With a knife or skewer placed down into both batters, trace a pattern of waves back and forth around the cake tin, to partially mix the two batters. Then lightly smooth down the surface of the mixture.

6. Place the tin on the middle shelf of the oven and bake for 30–35 minutes, or until a skewer inserted into the cake comes out clean. Leave the cake to cool for 10 minutes in its tin, before turning it out onto a wire rack to cool completely.

Try Something Different

To make the classic vanilla and chocolate tiger cake, just substitute ½ teaspoon of vanilla extract for the cinnamon. If you do not have a bundt tin you can bake this in a 900g loaf tin or a 23cm round cake tin and bake as above. Check for doneness after 30 minutes and return to the oven for a further 5–10 minutes if needed.

Easy does it

HANDS-ON TIME:
20 minutes

BAKING TIME:
30–35 minutes

MAKES:
1 large cake,
to serve 10–12

SPECIAL
EQUIPMENT:
25cm bundt tin or
cake ring, skewer

STORAGE:
Keep for up to
3 days in an airtight
container

Chocolate Truffle Cake

This indulgent dessert is essentially a whipped ganache, which makes it a giant truffle, hence the name. The only baking involved is for the biscuit base, although you could use shop-bought biscuits to make it even simpler.

⅓ quantity (150g) Cocoa Stars
(see page 48)
60g unsalted butter
450g 60–65 per cent dark chocolate
(Madagascan is ideal)
100ml maple syrup
3 tablespoons brandy
600ml whipping cream, well chilled

To decorate
50g white chocolate

Easy does it

HANDS-ON TIME:
30 minutes

SERVES:
12

SPECIAL
EQUIPMENT:
20cm springclip
cake tin

METHOD USED:
Melting chocolate,
page 24

STORAGE:
Keep for up to
1 week in the fridge

1. Follow the recipe on page 48 to make the Cocoa Stars and allow them to cool completely. You will only need about one-third of the biscuits the recipe makes but the leftover biscuits won't hang around for long!

2. Crush the chocolate biscuits to a rough crumb by placing them inside a plastic bag and bashing lightly. Melt the butter in a pan then remove from the heat and add the crushed biscuits. Combine the two thoroughly and then tip into the cake tin and press down to cover the base in an even layer. This will form the base of your truffle cake. Place in the fridge to chill while you get on with the truffle filling.

3. **Melt** the chocolate in a bain-marie: break the chocolate into pieces so that it has the best chance to melt evenly. Place in a heatproof bowl with the maple syrup and brandy and set this bowl over a pan of gently simmering water, making sure that the bottom of the bowl doesn't touch the water. Melt the contents of the bowl, stirring occasionally to bring them smoothly together.
Continued

4. Next in a large bowl whisk the 600ml cream until it is aerated and thickened. You don't want peaks, just a thick pouring consistency. Loosen the chocolate mixture by stirring in a couple of spoonfuls of the whipped cream. Then add the melted chocolate mixture to the rest of the cream and **fold** it through until you have a smooth, fully combined, thick chocolate cream.

5. Take the cake tin out of the fridge and pour the chocolate cream filling over the chilled base, smoothing down the top until it is roughly level. Return the truffle cake to the fridge to firm up overnight.

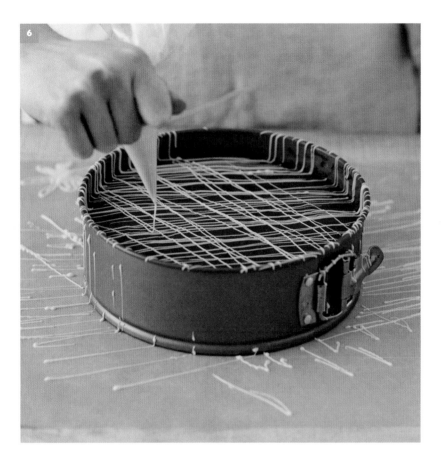

6. When the cake is set you can decorate it. Place the 50g white chocolate in a heatproof bowl to melt it, either set over a pan of gently simmering water (making sure the bottom of the bowl doesn't touch the water) or in the microwave. Use it to **fill** a small disposable piping bag and snip off the end to create a small hole. **Pipe** the chocolate straight away onto the cold cake. The cake should be cold enough to set the chocolate, but you can put it back in the fridge until you are ready to serve it.

7. Allow the truffle cake to come to room temperature for about 30 minutes before serving. **Remove the cake from its tin,** but serve it on the base, as it will be difficult to slide off.

Try Something Different

You could make the base with digestive biscuits (see White Chocolate-dipped Lemon Digestives, page 78); just leave out the lemon zest before baking.

White Chocolate-dipped Lemon Digestives

Making chocolate digestives yourself at home is easy to do and they are so delicious! Here the classic is given a lift with lemon zest and a white chocolate coating.

For the biscuits
100g plain white flour
100g plain wholemeal flour
100g porridge oats
75g muscovado sugar
½ teaspoon bicarbonate of soda
¾ teaspoon salt

zest of 1 unwaxed lemon
125g unsalted butter, cut into small cubes
3 tablespoons milk

To decorate
200g white chocolate

HANDS-ON TIME:
40 minutes

HANDS-OFF TIME:
30 minutes chilling

BAKING TIME:
10–12 minutes

MAKES:
24 biscuits

SPECIAL EQUIPMENT:
2 baking sheets,
6cm round cutter

METHOD USED:
Melting chocolate,
page 24

STORAGE:
Keep for up to
1 week in an airtight container

1. Put all of the dry ingredients into a large bowl, add the lemon zest and mix them together. Then add the butter and rub in with your fingers until it is fully worked through and the contents of the bowl resembles rough breadcrumbs. Lastly add the milk and bring it together into a soft dough.

2. Wrap the dough in clingfilm and place it in the fridge to chill for 30 minutes. While the dough is chilling preheat the oven to 190°C (170°C fan), 375°F, Gas 5 and line two baking sheets with baking paper.

3. Lightly flour a work surface and your rolling pin and **roll** the dough out to a thickness of about 4mm. Using the 6cm round cookie cutter, **cut** shapes out of the dough and place them a little apart on the prepared baking sheets. Gather together the off-cuts and re-roll to create more biscuits.

4. Bake the cookies for 10–12 minutes, or until they are golden at the edges. **Lift** the biscuits onto a wire rack; they will crisp up as they cool.

5. While the biscuits are cooling, **melt** the chocolate in a bain-marie. Break the white chocolate into chunks, so that it has the best chance to melt evenly. Place in a heatproof bowl set over a pan of gently simmering water, making sure that the bottom of the bowl doesn't touch the water. Stir to ensure it melts smoothly and evenly.

6. When the chocolate has melted, remove the bowl from the heat and set to one side. Carefully lift each biscuit at the edges and dip the top fully into the chocolate. Lift the biscuits out, and when they have stopped dripping, place them chocolate side up on a sheet of baking paper to allow the chocolate to set.

Try Something Different

To make a plain digestive just leave out the lemon zest. You could then coat them with milk or dark chocolate; melt the same amount of milk or dark chocolate as above.

Chocolate Soufflé

This is a simpler version of the classic impressive dessert – but it is still delicate and deeply flavoured. Make sure to fold the chocolate into the whisked egg whites until no egg white remains visible.

125g 70–75 per cent dark chocolate
2 tablespoons milk
75g caster sugar
4 medium egg yolks, at room temperature
6 medium egg whites, at room temperature
pinch of salt
double cream, to serve

1. Preheat the oven to 200°C (180°C fan), 400°F, Gas 6 and **butter** your soufflé dish.

2. **Melt** the chocolate in a bain-marie: break the chocolate into pieces, so that it has the best chance to melt evenly, and place in a heatproof bowl with the milk. Set the bowl over a pan of gently simmering water, making sure that the bottom of the bowl doesn't touch the water. Allow it to melt, stirring the chocolate and milk occasionally to mix them together. Remove the pan from the heat, place the bowl on your worktop and then beat in the sugar and egg yolks to form a smooth paste. Set to one side.

3. In a clean bowl **whisk** the egg whites with the salt until stiff peaks form when the whisk is removed. Loosen the chocolate mixture by beating in a good spoonful of the beaten egg whites. Next, using a spatula, gently **fold** the chocolate mixture into the remaining egg whites, just until no white patches of egg white remain visible.

4. Pour the mixture into your prepared dish and place the dish on a sheet on the middle shelf of the oven. Bake the soufflé for 20 minutes. When you take the soufflé out it will be puffed up and the top cracked. Serve the soufflé immediately with a jug of cold cream alongside.

Try Something Different

For a variation in flavour you could replace some or all of the milk with brandy. Or for a subtle orange flavour try freshly squeezed orange juice.

Easy does it

HANDS-ON TIME:
15 minutes

BAKING TIME:
20 minutes

SERVES:
4

SPECIAL EQUIPMENT:
18cm round soufflé dish, 9–10cm deep

METHOD USED:
Melting chocolate, page 24

STORAGE:
Best eaten immediately

Flourless Chocolate Cake

This dessert is both rich and airy, a cross between a chocolate fondant and a soufflé. It is simply made by folding whisked egg whites through the other melted ingredients. Serve warm with cold cream, crème fraîche or ice cream. It is also delicious chilled.

225g 65 per cent dark chocolate
125g unsalted butter, cut into small pieces
175g caster sugar
100ml boiling water
4 medium eggs, at room temperature, separated
pinch of salt
icing sugar, for dusting (optional)
physalis, to garnish (optional)

Easy does it

HANDS-ON TIME:
25 minutes

BAKING TIME:
35–45 minutes

SERVES:
10–12

SPECIAL EQUIPMENT:
23cm springclip cake tin, baking sheet

STORAGE:
Keep for up to 4 days in the fridge

1. Preheat the oven to 170°C (150°C fan), 325°F, Gas 3. **Butter** the cake tin and **line** the base with baking paper.

2. Finely chop the chocolate and place into a large mixing bowl with the butter and sugar. Pour the boiling water over and stir thoroughly until all is melted and well combined. If everything does not fully melt from the heat of the hot water you can set the bowl over a pan of gently simmering water, making sure the bottom of the bowl doesn't touch the water, or place in the microwave for a few seconds to complete the process. But be careful not to overheat.

3. Add the egg yolks and salt to the chocolate mixture and beat until they are fully mixed in.

4. In a clean bowl **whisk** the egg whites to stiff peaks. Next, using a large spatula, **fold** the egg whites into the chocolate mixture until they are fully mixed together.

5. Pour the mixture into the prepared tin, place the tin on a baking sheet and bake it in the oven for about 35–45 minutes. A skewer inserted into it will not come out fully clean, but neither do you want liquid raw mixture.

6. Take the cake out of the oven and place it in its tin on a wire rack to cool. The cake will be puffed up when it comes out of the oven, but will settle as it cools. Once it is cool **remove the cake from its tin**: run a sharp knife around the edge of the cake, unclip the side of the tin and lift it off. (As it is a fragile and mousse-like cake, it may be easier to serve it on the base.) Dust with icing sugar and serve with a physalis, if desired, and cream, crème fraîche or ice cream.

White Chocolate Baked Cheesecake

A creamy baked cheesecake with a biscuit base. The mixture is sweetened by the white chocolate, which contrasts well with the sharpness of the blackcurrants.

150g digestive biscuits (see page 78 or use shop-bought)
50g unsalted butter, melted
200g white chocolate, in chips or small pieces
50ml double cream
50ml milk

560g cream cheese
pinch of salt
2 medium eggs, at room temperature

For the blackcurrant sauce
400g blackcurrants, fresh or frozen
150g caster sugar

1. Preheat the oven to 160°C (140°C fan), 325°F, Gas 3 and lightly **butter** the cake tin.

2. Crush the digestive biscuits to fine crumbs by placing them inside a plastic bag and bashing lightly. Combine the crumbs with the melted butter and tip this mixture into your prepared cake tin. Press down into the base of the tin to form an even layer. Place the tin into the freezer while you make the filling. If you want to make the base the day before you could just leave it in the fridge. Putting it in the freezer allows it to set enough in the time it takes to make the filling.

3. To make the filling, place the chocolate into a heatproof bowl. Heat the double cream and milk in a pan over a medium heat until hot, but not boiling, before pouring it over the white chocolate. Let it sit for a moment, and then stir gently until you have smooth cream. The chocolate will melt in the heat of the cream and milk.

4. In a large bowl beat the cream cheese with the salt, adding in the eggs one at a time until you have a light, smooth mixture. Then stir in the melted white chocolate cream until everything is fully incorporated.

5. Take the base out of the freezer and pour the filling over the base, smoothing it level. Place the tin on a baking sheet and bake on the middle shelf of the oven for 1 hour, then turn the oven off, open the oven door, and leave the cheesecake inside for an hour, to allow it to set completely and cool. Transfer to a wire rack to cool fully in its tin. Refrigerate the cheesecake, still in its tin, for at least a few hours, or overnight. **Remove from the tin** but leave on the cake base to serve.

6. To make the blackcurrant sauce, place the blackcurrants and sugar in a pan, stir, and then bring to the boil before turning off the heat. Serve hot or cold alongside the cold cheesecake.

Try Something Different

You can serve this with any fruit or fruit sauce – something with a good level of acidity works best to offset the sweetness of the chocolate.

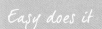

Easy does it

HANDS-ON TIME:
25 minutes

HANDS-OFF TIME:
Overnight chilling

BAKING TIME:
1 hour, plus 1 hour with oven off and door open

SERVES:
10

SPECIAL EQUIPMENT:
23cm springclip cake tin

STORAGE:
Keep for up to 5 days in the fridge

Chocolate Fondants

These 'tricky' desserts are actually very simple to make, and take very little time to prepare. The secret to a molten centre is in getting to know the precise cooking time for your oven. The only thing you need add to a fondant is cold cream to pour into it, or vanilla ice cream that will melt on top.

Easy does it

HANDS-ON TIME:
20 minutes,
plus optional chilling

BAKING TIME:
10–15 minutes

MAKES:
6 chocolate fondants

SPECIAL
EQUIPMENT:
6 × 200–225ml
ramekins, baking
sheet

METHOD USED:
Melting chocolate,
page 24

200g 60–65 per cent dark chocolate (Madagascan or Ecuadorian would work well)
150g unsalted butter

5 medium eggs, at room temperature
200g caster sugar
50g plain flour
pinch of salt

1. **Butter and flour** the ramekins and set them onto a baking sheet.

2. Break the chocolate into pieces and place with the butter in a small pan over a very low heat. Keep an eye on it, stirring occasionally and breaking up the butter into smaller pieces, to **melt** the butter and chocolate together. Set them to one side to cool a little.

3. Put the eggs and sugar into a large bowl and **whisk** them together until they are light and airy. Next pour in the chocolate mixture and continue whisking until everything is fully mixed together. Lastly **fold** in the flour and salt until they are just combined.

4. Pour the chocolate fondant mixture equally between the ramekins and put them into the fridge until needed. They can wait for a few hours, or until the following day, although you can bake them straight away if your oven is preheated. They even respond well to freezing; wrap each ramekin well in clingfilm and freeze for up to 3 months. You can then defrost them, or bake them from frozen if you give them about 5 minutes' extra cooking time.

5. Preheat the oven to 200°C (180°C fan), 400°F, Gas 6 well in advance of when you are ready to eat the fondants so that it is fully hot.

6. Bake the fondants on their baking sheet for about 15 minutes, but start checking after 10 minutes, watching carefully for when to take them out. The secret to their molten centres is to bake them only to the point when the outside is set, but the inside remains liquid. You can judge this by looking at their tops. As soon as they are puffed up and the tops begin to crack they are done. Before this you will still be able to see dark uncooked mixture on top. If you leave them in for longer after they have just risen and cracked they will cook throughout. Serve the fondants immediately.

Try Something Different

If you do end up with over-baked fondants, don't worry, you will still have tasty hot chocolate sponge! Serve with plenty of ice cream alongside as they won't be as moist as a proper fondant.

Prune and Dark Chocolate Kugelhopf

This brioche-like sweet bread uses yeast to make it rise and is loaded with the delicious combination of prunes and dark chocolate. It is classically baked in a characteristic patterned ring mould.

200ml milk
2 sachets (14g) fast-action dried yeast
100g caster sugar
600g strong white bread flour
1 teaspoon salt
4 medium eggs, at room temperature
1 teaspoon vanilla extract

200g unsalted butter, softened
200g soft prunes, stoned and cut into large chunks
150g 60–70 per cent dark chocolate chips or chunks
icing sugar, for dusting

Easy does it

HANDS-ON TIME:
30 minutes

HANDS-OFF TIME:
3½ hours proving

BAKING TIME:
35–40 minutes

MAKES:
16 slices

SPECIAL EQUIPMENT:
25cm kugelhopf or bundt tin

STORAGE:
Best eaten the day you make it, or keep for up to 3 days in an airtight container

1. Firstly, warm the milk a little in a pan, just to body temperature (it should feel neither hot nor cold to the touch), and then add the yeast and the sugar.

2. Put the flour and salt into a large bowl, or the bowl of a free-standing mixer fitted with a dough hook. This is a wet dough, so it is easier to knead in a mixer than by hand if you do have that option. Mix the flour and salt together briefly, then continue to mix while adding the milk mixture, bringing the flour into the liquid to incorporate. Continue to knead the dough, adding the eggs one by one, and knead for about 10 minutes until you have a well-mixed, loose dough.

3. Still kneading, add the butter a little at a time, until it is all mixed in. Knead this for another few minutes. Then cover the bowl with clingfilm and leave it to rise in a warm place for about 2 hours, or until doubled in size.

4. **Butter** your kugelhopf or bundt tin well. When the dough is risen, turn it out onto a floured surface and knock it back by punching it lightly into a flat disc; this removes any large air bubbles that may have formed and helps to create an

even texture. Scatter the prunes and chocolate over the flat dough and then knead it back in on itself, just enough to mix the fruit and chocolate evenly into the dough. Form the dough into a flat round and make a hole in the centre with your thumbs. Lift the dough carefully, and drop it down into your tin, with the central part of the tin coming up through the hole in your dough. Cover with clingfilm and let rise for about 1½ hours, until doubled in size.

5. Preheat the oven to 190°C (170°C fan), 375°F, Gas 5. Bake the kugelhopf in the oven for 35–40 minutes, by which time it should be risen and golden. Allow it to cool in the tin for a few minutes before turning out onto a wire rack to cool. Dust the kugelhopf with icing sugar before slicing and serving.

Try Something Different

Use different combinations of chocolate and dried fruit, or add nuts. A traditional kugelhopf is topped with almonds: just scatter toasted slivered almonds into the mould before you put the dough in for its second rise.

Raspberry and Dark Chocolate Mousse Cake

A dessert-worthy cake that starts with a mousse. Half of the mousse is baked, and the other half is spread on top once it has cooled. Raspberries go particularly well with chocolate: here they are baked within and also served alongside in a ripple cream.

HANDS-ON TIME:
35 minutes

HANDS-OFF TIME:
2–3 hours cooling

BAKING TIME:
20 minutes

SERVES:
6

SPECIAL EQUIPMENT:
20cm loose-bottomed cake tin

METHOD USED:
Melting chocolate, page 24

STORAGE:
Keep for 2–3 days in the fridge

For the cake
150g 60–65 per cent dark chocolate (Madagascan would work well)
150g unsalted butter
3 medium eggs, at room temperature, separated
100g caster sugar
pinch of salt

2 rounded tablespoons plain flour
1 teaspoon baking powder
125g fresh raspberries

For the raspberry ripple cream
200g raspberries
35g sugar
300ml double cream, well chilled

1. Preheat the oven to 200°C (180°C fan), 400°F, Gas 6 and **butter and flour** your cake tin.

2. Break the chocolate into small pieces and **melt** with the butter in a small pan over a very low heat until just melted, stirring occasionally to mix the two together. Next, put the egg yolks and sugar in a small bowl and use a rubber spatula to make a paste, so that the sugar is mostly dissolved. Then beat the egg yolk mixture into the melted chocolate.

3. **Whisk** the egg whites with the salt in a large bowl until it forms stiff peaks. Then **fold** the chocolate mixture into the egg whites until they are fully combined.

4. Divide the mixture in two and chill one half. Add the flour and baking powder to the remaining half, fold it carefully through the mousse, and pour the mixture into the prepared cake tin. Arrange the raspberries on top of the cake mixture and bake for 20 minutes,

or until a skewer comes out clean. Allow the cake to cool completely in the tin, for 2–3 hours.

5. When the cake is cold **remove from the tin** and place it on a serving plate. Spread the remaining mousse on the top.

6. To make the raspberry cream, crush the raspberries and sugar together with a fork. Then whip the cream to soft peaks and swirl the two together with a few strokes for a ripple effect. Serve the raspberry ripple cream alongside slices of the cake.

Try Something Different

You can make this without the raspberries for a plain two-layered mousse cake, in which case you should reduce the cooking time by about 5 minutes.

Dark Chocolate Ganache Tart

A butter-smooth dark chocolate **ganache** set inside crisp sweet pastry – two techniques well worth mastering. The chocolate you use here will transform the result, so it is worth choosing carefully.

HANDS-ON TIME:
35 minutes

HANDS-OFF TIME:
1 hour chilling

BAKING TIME:
25 minutes

MAKES:
16–20 slices

METHOD USED:
Chocolate ganache,
page 26

SPECIAL EQUIPMENT:
25cm fluted loose-bottomed tart tin

STORAGE:
Keep for up to 4 days in the fridge

For the sweet pastry (pâte sucrée)

125g unsalted butter, at room temperature
100g icing sugar
250g plain flour
pinch of salt
2 medium egg yolks, at room temperature
2 tablespoons cold milk

For the ganache filling

500g 60–65 per cent dark chocolate, preferably something bright and fruity
350ml double cream
50g golden syrup
pinch of salt
75g unsalted butter, cut into small pieces
75ml cold milk

1. To make the sweet **pastry**, cream the butter and sugar in a large bowl with a wooden spoon. Next mix in the flour and salt lightly with a spoon, then rub in with your fingertips or cut in with two round-bladed knives in a crossing action, until the mixture resembles fine breadcrumbs. Whisk the egg yolks and milk together and then add to the bowl, cutting in until just combined and you feel that the pastry would come together if pressed. (Or make the pastry in a food-processor.)

2. Turn the pastry out onto a lightly floured surface, and bring it together with floured hands, handling it as little as possible. Shape the dough into a flat disc, wrap it in clingfilm and chill in the fridge for at least 30 minutes.

3. **Roll** the pastry out on your floured surface to a disc a bit larger than your tart tin, about 30cm in diameter and just thicker than a £1 coin. Use it to **line** the tin, easing the pastry into the corners and pressing it into the flutes of the tin. Trim the pastry edges (wrap and keep the excess pastry for patching up any cracks). Lightly prick the base with a fork and chill for a further 30 minutes. Preheat the oven to 190°C (170°C fan), 375°F, Gas 5.
Continued

4. Line the pastry case with baking paper and fill with baking beans or uncooked rice. **Blind bake** for 15 minutes, then remove the beans and paper. If necessary, patch up any pastry cracks and bake for a further 10 minutes, or until golden brown and the base feels sandy to the touch. (The tart case needs to be fully cooked when you have finished, as it will not be baked again.) Leave the tart case to cool completely, as you do not want to fill it while it is warm.

5. To make the ganache filling, break the 500g chocolate into pieces and put into a large mixing bowl. Put the 350ml cream, 50g golden syrup and pinch of salt in a pan and heat to just below boiling point. Pour the hot cream mixture over the chocolate and stir to melt, making a **ganache**. Then add the 75g butter and stir until it has also melted. Lastly add the 75ml cold milk and whisk the mixture until it is smooth and glossy.

6. Pour the ganache filling into the baked tart case and smooth the surface with a spatula. Allow the tart to cool and set for a couple of hours at room temperature before serving. It is also good served from the fridge, if a little firmer.

Sablé Kisses

These tender cookies are sandwiched together with a home-made chocolate hazelnut spread. You will need a food-processor to make it, but it is easy to do. You will also have plenty of spread left over, but it is hard to process if you try and make small quantities. Keep it in the fridge and spread on crusty white bread.

HANDS-ON TIME:
50 minutes

HANDS-OFF TIME:
1 hour chilling

BAKING TIME:
10–12 minutes

MAKES:
28 sandwich biscuits

SPECIAL EQUIPMENT:
Food-processor, 4cm heart-shaped cutter, 2 baking sheets

STORAGE:
Keep for up to 1 week in an airtight container in the fridge

For the chocolate hazelnut spread
100g hazelnuts
50ml milk
50ml double cream
2 tablespoons golden syrup
100g milk chocolate, broken into chunks
30g 70 per cent dark chocolate, broken into chunks
pinch of salt
3 tablespoons skimmed milk powder

For the almond sablé biscuits
125g unsalted butter, softened
100g caster sugar
1 medium egg, at room temperature
125g plain flour
100g ground almonds
½ teaspoon salt
½ teaspoon baking powder

1. To make the chocolate hazelnut spread, place the hazelnuts in a food-processor and grind to a fine powder. Place the milk, cream and golden syrup in a small pan and heat to just below boiling point, stirring once.

2. Add the milk chocolate and dark chocolate to the food-processor along with the salt and skimmed milk powder, and process until it is finely chopped into the ground nuts. Then, with the motor still running, pour over the hot milk mixture. The heat of the milk will melt the chocolate. Continue to process, stopping to scrape down the sides of the bowl if necessary to ensure everything is evenly combined, until you have a smooth mixture. Then pour the hazelnut chocolate spread into a bowl or jar to cool.

3. To make the biscuits, cream the butter and sugar together until light and fluffy. Then beat in the egg. Combine the flour, ground almonds, salt and baking powder in another bowl, then **fold** them into the butter mixture. Mix just enough to bring it together into a dough. You will need floured hands to do this as it is a very soft dough. Wrap the dough in clingfilm and chill it in the fridge for 1 hour.

4. Preheat the oven to 180°C (160°C fan), 350°F, Gas 4 and line two baking sheets with baking paper.
Continued

5. **Roll** the dough out on a floured surface to a thickness of about 5mm. Use a heart-shaped cutter to **cut out** your shapes and place them a little apart on the baking sheets. You will need to flour your rolling pin and cutter well to prevent the dough from sticking.

6. Bake the biscuits for around 10–12 minutes, or until they are lightly golden. Allow them to cool on the baking sheets for a minute to firm up a little. **Lift** the biscuits from the baking sheet and transfer them to a wire rack to cool completely.

7. When your biscuits are cold, sandwich pairs together with the chocolate hazelnut spread, which will have thickened to a spreading consistency as it cooled.

Almond, Macadamia
and Orange Florentines

These patisserie classics don't take long to make, but need a little care in handling as they firm up quickly after baking. Coat them with white, milk or dark chocolate, all of which go well with nuts and a hint of orange.

vegetable oil, for greasing
30g unsalted butter
75g caster sugar
1 tablespoon golden syrup
30g plain flour
100ml double cream
100g flaked almonds
100g macadamia nuts, roughly chopped
zest of 1 orange
150g chocolate of your choice

1. Preheat the oven to 180°C (160°C fan), 350°F, Gas 4 and lightly grease your baking sheets with vegetable oil.

2. To make the Florentine mixture put the butter, sugar and syrup in a medium pan and melt them together over a low heat. Next, taking the pan off the heat, add the flour and cream and whisk everything together until smooth.

3. Add all the nuts and the orange zest to the contents of the pan. Then stir everything together thoroughly, making sure that it is evenly mixed and all the nuts are well coated.

Continued

Needs a little skill

HANDS-ON TIME:
35 minutes

BAKING TIME:
10–12 minutes

MAKES:
16 Florentines

SPECIAL EQUIPMENT:
2 baking sheets, spatula or palette knife

METHOD USED:
Melting chocolate, page 24

STORAGE:
Keep in an airtight container for up to 3 days

4. Spoon the mixture into small mounds, spaced well apart, on your greased baking sheets (they will spread in the oven). Pat them down a little with the back of the spoon. You want the nuts in just one layer, rather than piled on top of each other.

5. Put the baking sheets into the oven and bake the Florentines for about 10–12 minutes, until they are golden at the edges. When you take them out you won't be able to transfer them immediately to a wire rack, as they will be too delicate. But do so the minute you are able to, as if you leave them too long they will harden and become more difficult to move. When they are just firm enough to lift, after about 1 minute, ease a spatula or palette knife under each one in turn, working carefully but quickly, as the rest will continue to harden. It will help to use a lightly greased metal spatula or palette knife. Place them carefully on wire racks and leave the Florentines to cool completely before coating with the chocolate.

6. **Melt** the chocolate in a bain-marie. Break the 150g chocolate into pieces, so that it has the best chance to melt evenly, and put into a heatproof bowl set over a pan of gently simmering water, making sure the bottom of the bowl doesn't touch the water. Alternatively use a microwave. Stir until smooth, remove from the heat and leave to cool slightly. Using a pastry brush, paint the underside of each Florentine with the melted chocolate. Lay each Florentine chocolate side up on a sheet of baking paper. Leave all the Florentines for about 30 minutes so that the chocolate is completely set before serving.

Try Something Different

You can mix up the nuts you use and add in candied peel and glacé cherries if you like them. Just make sure the total amount of fruit and nuts is 200g, or you may not have enough mixture to coat them.

Flourless Chocolate and Almond Cake

This gluten-free cake is easy to put together and is a perfect pudding cake, served with forest fruits and a white chocolate sauce. Lots of dark chocolate is **melted** and stirred through whisked eggs and ground almonds.

Needs a little skill

HANDS-ON TIME:
15 minutes

BAKING TIME:
30–35 minutes

SERVES:
12

SPECIAL EQUIPMENT:
23cm loose-bottomed cake tin

METHOD USED:
Melting chocolate, page 24

STORAGE:
Keep for up to 1 week in the fridge

For the cake
200g unsalted butter
200g 60–65 per cent dark chocolate (Ecuadorian would suit this recipe)
5 medium eggs, at room temperature
200g caster sugar
150g ground almonds
pinch of salt

For the white chocolate sauce
150g white chocolate
150ml double cream
25g unsalted butter
50ml milk

To serve
200g fresh forest fruits

1. To make the cake, preheat the oven to 180°C (160°C fan), 350°F, Gas 4. Grease and **line** the base of your cake tin.

2. Put the butter and chocolate into a small pan and **melt** them slowly over a low heat, stirring occasionally and breaking the butter into smaller pieces, to melt them together.

3. Put the eggs and sugar into a large bowl and whisk them well until they are light, fluffy and pale. Keep whisking as you pour in the melted chocolate mixture. Lastly **fold** in the ground almonds and salt until you have a smooth batter.

4. Pour your cake batter into the prepared cake tin and bake it on the middle shelf of the oven for 30 minutes. To test for doneness, insert a skewer into the centre of the cake. It will not come out completely clean, as this is a moist cake and you should see some moist crumb. If you still see lots of raw liquid mixture return the cake to the oven for a further 5 minutes. When the cake is done place it in its tin on a wire rack to cool completely.

5. To make the white chocolate sauce, melt the white chocolate and cream together in a heatproof bowl set over a pan of gently simmering water, making sure the bottom of the bowl doesn't touch the water. When the chocolate has completely melted, take off the heat and beat in the butter. Once they are fully mixed together add the milk and beat it in. Pour it into a jug and then set the sauce to one side until you are ready to serve the cake. It will thicken as it cools but you can reheat the sauce gently if you want to serve it warm. To serve, **remove the cake from its tin** and cut into slices. Serve each slice with some forest fruits and pour over the white chocolate sauce.

Try Something Different

You can vary the nuts you use to make the cake: just swap in the same weight of any nuts you prefer and grind them finely before using. Hazelnuts are particularly good. If you **roast** the nuts before grinding them they will have a more intense flavour.

Steamed Chocolate
Sponge with Chocolate
Custard

A burst of nostalgia with this school pudding classic, but home-made it is so much better! The simple sponge is rich with cocoa and moist from steaming, and served with custard flavoured with melted chocolate.

For the sponge
100g unsalted butter, softened
150g caster sugar
2 medium eggs, at room temperature
200g self-raising flour
pinch of salt
25g cocoa powder
100ml milk

For the custard
600ml whipping cream
6 medium egg yolks
20g sugar
100g 70–75 per cent dark chocolate
(Grenadan would be ideal)

Needs a little skill

HANDS-ON TIME:
45 minutes

COOKING TIME:
2 hours

SERVES:
8–10

SPECIAL EQUIPMENT:
1-litre pudding basin

STORAGE:
Best eaten the day you make it. You can make the custard up to 2 days in advance and keep in the fridge with clingfilm on the surface to prevent a skin forming

1. **Butter** the pudding basin well and place a disc of baking paper inside to cover the base. Then butter the disc as well.

2. To make the sponge, cream the butter and sugar together until the mixture is light and fluffy. Then beat in the eggs, one at a time.

3. Mix the flour with the salt, and sift the cocoa powder over the flour before mixing them all together. Add the flour and cocoa to the butter, sugar and egg mixture and **fold** it through thoroughly. Lastly add the milk, and continue folding until you have a smooth batter.
Continued

4. Pour the sponge batter into the prepared pudding basin. Take a large circle of baking paper or foil, and fold a pleat in the centre to allow room for the sponge to rise. Place this on top of the pudding basin to cover it and secure the foil well with string.

5. Place the pudding basin in a large, deep pan on a trivet or upturned saucer. Pour boiling water to halfway up the side of the pudding basin, and remember to top it up during the cooking time to prevent it boiling dry. Cover with a tight-fitting lid: a good way of ensuring this is to cover the pan with foil and then add the lid. Simmer the sponge over a low heat for 2 hours. Then remove the basin from the pan to a wire rack to cool a little before turning out the sponge onto your serving plate.

6. While the sponge is steaming you can make the custard. Put the 600ml cream into a pan to warm through over a low heat. Whisk the 6 egg yolks and 20g sugar together in a heatproof bowl. Then pour the warm cream onto the eggs and sugar, whisking all the time. Next pour the custard mixture back into the pan and cook, stirring continuously over a low heat, until the custard has thickened to your desired consistency. This will take 10–15 minutes, depending on how high your heat.

7. Put the 100g chocolate into the bowl that held the eggs and sugar, and when your custard is thickened pour it over the chocolate. Stir the custard through until the chocolate has melted into it and you have a smooth chocolate custard.

8. Serve the chocolate sponge with the custard; both the sponge and custard are delicious hot or cold.

Try Something Different

To make a white chocolate custard just substitute the dark chocolate in the custard recipe for the same amount of white chocolate.

Chocolate Éclairs

Chocolate éclairs are too wonderful to ever go out of favour. The combination of puffed choux pastry shell, smooth chocolate crème pâtissière and chocolate coating is a heavenly one that you can easily make at home.

Needs a little skill

HANDS-ON TIME:
1¼ hours

BAKING TIME:
35 minutes

MAKES:
20 medium éclairs

SPECIAL EQUIPMENT:
2 baking sheets,
2 piping bags, 1cm
plain round piping
nozzle, 4mm plain
round piping nozzle

METHOD USED:
Melting chocolate,
page 24

STORAGE:
Keep the filled and
coated éclairs for 2–3
days in the fridge.
Unfilled éclairs will
keep for up to
1 week in an airtight
container or can
be frozen for up to
2 months

For the choux pastry
50g unsalted butter, cut into small pieces
125ml water
75g plain flour
3 medium eggs, at room temperature

For the crème pâtissière
2 medium eggs
1 medium egg yolk

125g caster sugar
2 tablespoons cocoa powder
170ml milk
230ml whipping cream, well chilled

For the coating
200g milk chocolate, broken into pieces
50g white or dark chocolate, to decorate (optional)

1. To make the choux pastry shells, preheat the oven to 200°C (180°C fan), 400°F, Gas 6 and line two baking sheets with baking paper.

2. Put the butter and water together in a small pan, and ensure you have your other ingredients measured and ready to hand. Also prepare a piping bag with a 1cm plain round piping nozzle. Heat the water and butter to boiling point, and then remove from the heat and add the flour and beat it together to create a smooth paste. Then put the pan back over a medium heat and cook for a minute or two, stirring until the paste forms a glossy ball. Then take the mixture back off the heat.

3. Next you need to beat in the eggs, one by one. This is most easily done in a free-standing mixer fitted with the beater attachment, but it can be done by hand with plenty of elbow grease. If you are going to use a mixer tip the dough into the bowl and start beating the dough without adding the eggs for a minute or two; this allows it to dry out a little, making it more absorbent for the eggs. Then add the eggs one at a time, making sure each is fully incorporated before adding the next. Keep beating until you have a very smooth mixture. It should be glossy and of a very thick pouring consistency. *Continued*

4. **Fill** your piping bag with the choux pastry and **pipe** even lines on the lined baking sheets, approximately 10cm long and spaced well apart.

5. Bake the éclair shells for 35 minutes without opening the oven door, and then take the trays out and allow them to cool completely.

6. To make the chocolate crème pâtissière, place the 2 eggs, 1 egg yolk, 125g caster sugar and 2 tablespoons of cocoa powder in a small pan and whisk them together off the heat until smooth. Then pour in the 170ml milk and 230ml cream and place over a low heat. Cook, stirring continuously, until the cream is well thickened. This may take

up to 20 minutes, depending on how cautious you are with the heat. When the crème pâtissière has thickened to the consistency of mayonnaise, pour it into a clean bowl, place clingfilm directly onto the surface to cover and prevent a skin forming, and put it in the fridge to cool down.

7. For the coating, **melt** the chocolate in a bain-marie. Place the 200g milk chocolate into a heatproof bowl (wide enough to dip the éclairs in) and set the bowl over a pan of gently simmering water, making sure the base of the bowl doesn't touch the water. Alternatively you can melt the chocolate in a microwave. Gently stir until it is completely smooth.

8. Pierce a hole into one end of each éclair shell with the 4mm plain round piping nozzle. Then fit the nozzle into a new piping bag and fill it with the chocolate crème pâtissière. Pipe in through each éclair to fill it up.

9. Dip the top of each filled éclair into the melted milk chocolate. When you have completed all your éclairs place them in the fridge for the chocolate to firm up.

10. If you want to decorate the éclairs, melt the 50g contrasting white or dark chocolate as above and place it into a disposable piping bag. Snip the end into a fine point and pipe lines back and forth across the set milk chocolate topping.

Try Something Different

The chocolate coating can be made with the same amount of white or dark chocolate.

To make a vanilla crème pâtissière replace the cocoa powder with a teaspoon of vanilla extract.

Chocolate Ice Cream Sandwiches

Making home-made ice cream is an easy skill to master and is a fantastic way to use up all those odd bits of leftover chocolate at Easter. Here milk chocolate ice cream is sandwiched between sugar cookies.

For the ice cream
600ml whipping cream
6 medium egg yolks
250g 35 per cent minimum milk chocolate, broken into pieces
2 tablespoons brandy

For the sugar cookies
125g unsalted butter
220g caster sugar
1 medium egg, at room temperature
½ teaspoon vanilla extract
175g plain flour
½ teaspoon bicarbonate of soda
½ teaspoon salt

1. To make the ice cream, put the cream into a medium pan and heat until just below boiling point. Beat the egg yolks in a heatproof bowl. Then pour the hot cream over the egg yolks, whisking as you do so. Return the cream mixture to the pan and cook over a low heat, stirring, for about 10 minutes, or until slightly thickened.

2. Next, take the pan off the heat and add the chocolate. Stir the mixture until all the chocolate has melted and is mixed in thoroughly. When it is cool, add the brandy and stir to mix it in.

3. Freeze your ice cream. If you have an ice cream machine, it will churn the mixture as it freezes – follow the manufacturer's instructions and then transfer to a plastic container with a good airtight lid and store in the freezer until needed. To freeze ice cream without a machine, transfer the mixture to a wide plastic container with an airtight lid. You need the mixture to be no deeper than about 5cm, so you can beat it easily. Place in the freezer.

After 1 hour remove the container and beat the mixture well, preferably with a hand-held electric mixer. Repeat this process twice more, at intervals of 1–1½ hours. Leave the ice cream in the freezer for at least 1 hour after the final beating, or until you are ready to serve.

4. When you are ready to make the sugar cookies, preheat the oven to 190° (170°C fan), 375°F, Gas 5 and lightly **butter** your baking sheets. *Continued*

HANDS-ON TIME:
45 minutes

HANDS-OFF TIME:
Ice cream chilling and freezing

BAKING TIME:
8 minutes

MAKES:
12 ice cream sandwiches

SPECIAL EQUIPMENT:
3 baking sheets (or 1 sheet and bake the cookies in batches)

STORAGE:
Both the ice cream and assembled sandwiches will keep in the freezer for up to 3 months

5. In a large bowl cream the 125g butter and 220g sugar, adding the sugar a little at a time, until it is light and fluffy. Next beat in the 1 medium egg and ½ teaspoon vanilla extract. Mix the 175g flour, ½ teaspoon bicarbonate of soda and ½ teaspoon salt together and then stir them into the butter, sugar and egg mixture.

6. Use a teaspoon to drop scoops of the batter onto the greased baking sheets, spaced well apart, or use one baking sheet and bake the cookies in batches. You should manage about eight cookies per tray on three trays, making 24 cookies.

7. Bake the cookies for about 8 minutes, or until golden at the edges. Leave the cookies on the baking sheets for just a minute or so to firm a little, then **lift** them with a metal spatula and place on a wire rack or a sheet of greaseproof paper on your work surface to cool.

8. When the cookies are cold take the ice cream out of the freezer to soften for about 10 minutes. Arrange the cookies into roughly matching pairs. Next scoop some of the ice cream onto one half of a pair of cookies and sandwich with the other cookie. Wrap each sandwich in foil or clingfilm as you go and place it in the freezer until you are ready to serve. Continue sandwiching cookies until you have used up all your ice cream and cookies.

Try Something Different

You can make these sandwiches with any ice cream you choose.
If you add 150g chocolate chips to the cookie dough before baking you can make chocolate chip ice cream sandwiches – or just eat the chocolate chip cookies on their own.

Fresh Mint
Ganache Truffles
in Dark Chocolate

Building on skills used to make the Simple Chocolate Truffles on page 52, these truffles take it a little further. Here the cream is infused with mint, and the truffles are **enrobed** with **tempered** chocolate.

For the ganache
150ml double cream
25 fresh mint leaves
150g 60–70 per cent dark chocolate
(Ecuadorian would work well)
25g butter, diced

To enrobe the truffles
300g dark chocolate (as above)

HANDS-ON TIME:
1¼ hours

HANDS-OFF TIME:
1 hour chilling

MAKES:
20–40 truffles,
depending on size

SPECIAL EQUIPMENT:
20cm square cake tin
(optional), kitchen
thermometer,
dipping fork
(optional)

METHOD USED:
Chocolate ganache,
page 26. Tempering
chocolate, page
29. Enrobing with
chocolate, page 32

STORAGE:
Keep in an airtight
container for up to
10 days

1. To make the **ganache**, put the cream in a pan with the mint leaves and place over a medium heat. Bring to just below boiling point, then set the cream to one side to infuse for about 30 minutes before straining it back into the pan to remove the mint leaves.

2. Make sure your chocolate is broken up into small pieces, so that it has the best chance to melt evenly. Then put the chocolate into a heatproof bowl. Bring the infused cream back up to a steaming temperature, before pouring the hot cream over the chocolate. Stir the cream gently to melt the chocolate, gradually incorporating all the chocolate into the cream to make a ganache.

3. When the chocolate is fully melted add the butter and beat into the ganache until it is all smoothly amalgamated. Line the square cake tin with clingfilm and pour the ganache into it, or leave in its bowl if you want to hand roll your chocolates. Place the ganache into the fridge for at least 1 hour to chill and harden.

4. When you are ready to form the truffles, either **cut the ganache** into cubes or rectangles (if you set it in a square cake tin), or scoop spoonfuls out of the bowl with a teaspoon and **roll the ganache** into balls between your hands. Place these back in the fridge to remain cool and firm while you **temper** your chocolate for enrobing.

5. Before you begin tempering ensure you have everything else ready, so that you can make the most of the period of time when the chocolate is at the optimum temperature. Cover your work surface with enough baking paper to receive the finished chocolates while they set and set a wire rack on top.
Continued

6. To temper the 300g chocolate, place 210g of it in a heatproof bowl over a pan of barely simmering water. Using your kitchen thermometer, measure the temperature of the chocolate as it melts. Stir it to ensure the heat is evenly distributed and do not allow it to get above 45–50°C (113–122°F). Take the bowl off the heat, and continue to stir to melt any remaining pieces of chocolate. Then add the remaining 90g of chocolate and stir this into the melted chocolate. Keep stirring as the newly added chocolate melts and the temperature comes down. Keep checking the temperature of the chocolate: you want it to reach 28–29°C (82.4–84.2°F). When it has come down to the correct temperature, place the bowl back over the simmering water very

briefly, keeping a watchful eye on the temperature. You want it to come back up to 32°C (89°F), but no higher. Bear in mind that the temperature will rise quickly, and continue to rise once you have removed the bowl from the heat.

7. When the chocolate is at 33°C (91°F) leave the bowl off the heat, dip a knife into the molten chocolate and scrape off one side on the edge of the bowl. Allow the remaining chocolate on the knife to set to test if it has been successfully tempered. Pop the knife in the fridge to allow the remaining chocolate on the knife to set. Touch the set chocolate very lightly – if it feels smooth and dry and doesn't take the impression of your fingertip then it is tempered.

8. When you have a bowl of tempered chocolate you need to work quickly to **enrobe** the truffles, as the longer you take, the thicker the chocolate will become as it cools. Using a large fork, dip each truffle into the molten chocolate to cover.

9. Lift the truffle out, allow the excess chocolate to drip off, and then place the chocolate on the wire rack to set.
If you have round ganache balls and you want to use your hands, you can roll the truffles between your hands with some of the tempered chocolate to coat them. Be warned: this will be messy! If you like you can wear fine disposable gloves. Allow the chocolate coating to set completely before transferring the chocolates to a box or plate.

Key Lime
Jaffa Cakes

Definitely more of a cake than a biscuit, this is a twist on the classic teatime treat. An almond financier base is topped with delicate fresh lime jelly and covered in thick dark chocolate. A tart tray is ideal but if you don't have one you can use a muffin tin – the biscuits may be a slightly different shape but still just as tasty.

For the jelly
5 sheets of leaf gelatine
125ml freshly squeezed lime juice (about 3½ limes)
75ml freshly squeezed orange juice (about 1 medium orange)
45g lime marmalade
100g caster sugar

For the cake bases
85g unsalted butter
60g ground almonds
70g icing sugar
20g plain flour
2 medium egg whites, at room temperature
½ teaspoon vanilla extract

For the chocolate coating
150g 60–65 per cent dark chocolate (Madagascan would be perfect)
10ml sunflower oil
lime zest to garnish (optional)

1. First make the jelly. Put the leaf gelatine in a bowl of cold water to soak for 10 minutes, until soft and floppy. Line the square cake tin or similar sized dish with clingfilm.

2. Put the lime juice, orange juice, marmalade and sugar together into a small pan and heat gently to dissolve the sugar and melt the marmalade. Bring to the boil and then remove from the heat. Lift the softened gelatine leaves from the cold water and squeeze gently to remove the excess water, then add to the hot liquid in the pan, stirring until they have melted completely. Pour the liquid through a strainer into the clingfilm-lined tin and place it in the fridge to set for at least 4 hours or preferably overnight.

3. To make the cake bases, preheat the oven to 170°C (150°C fan), 325°F, Gas 3 and **butter** the holes of the tart tray well.

4. First put the butter in a small pan and melt it over a medium heat to make a beurre noisette. This means leaving it over the heat after melting until it deepens in colour to pale brown, loses its milky smell and smells lightly nutty. Once you have reached this stage take the butter off the heat and leave it to cool a little.
Continued

Needs a little skill

HANDS-ON TIME:
50 minutes

HANDS-OFF TIME:
4 hours or overnight for the jelly to set

BAKING TIME
15–20 minutes

MAKES:
12 jaffa cakes

SPECIAL EQUIPMENT:
12-hole tart tray, 18cm square cake tin, 4cm round cutter

METHOD USED:
Melting chocolate, page 24

STORAGE:
Keep for up to 3 days in an airtight container or the fridge

5. Mix together the 60g ground almonds, 70g icing sugar and 20g flour. It is best to do this in a jug, as the mixture will be very wet when finished and it will be easier to pour it into the tart tray. Add the melted butter to the dry ingredients and mix until it is fully incorporated. Lastly add the 2 egg whites and ½ teaspoon of vanilla extract and mix well.

6. Pour the mixture evenly between the holes in your tart tray; it will only fill them by a third to a half. Bake the cake bases in the oven for 15–20 minutes, or until they have risen and are golden brown. Then turn the cakes out to cool on a wire rack.

7. Once your jelly is set and your cakes are cold, cut circles out of the jelly with a 4cm round cutter. Then use a palette knife to carefully lift one onto the top of each cake.

8. To make the chocolate coating for the jaffa cakes **melt** the chocolate in a bain-marie. Break the 150g chocolate into pieces and place in a heatproof bowl with the 10ml sunflower oil. Set the bowl over a pan of gently simmering water, making sure that the bottom of the bowl doesn't touch the water. Stir until it is completely smooth and then remove from the heat and leave to cool for a few minutes. Spoon the chocolate mixture over to cover the jelly and tops of each cake, ensuring that it completely covers the top and sides of each jelly so that it is fixed to the cake. Leave the cakes in a cool place to allow the chocolate to set fully before eating. You can garnish with a little lime zest just before serving.

Try Something Different

To make a more traditional jaffa cake, make a sponge cake base and swap the lime jelly for all orange.

Pains au Chocolat

An essential part of any continental breakfast and a great reason to start the day with chocolate! It is worth mastering this simpler 'rough' version of a yeast-risen croissant dough.

50ml milk, at room temperature
2 tablespoons warm water
1 medium egg, at room temperature
175g strong white flour
7g (1 sachet) fast-action dried yeast
1 tablespoon caster sugar
½ teaspoon salt
125g cold butter, cut into 4–5 pieces
100g dark chocolate
beaten egg, to glaze

1. To make the croissant dough, whisk the milk, water and egg together in a jug. Then put the flour, yeast, sugar, salt and butter into a large bowl and 'cut' them together to mix and break up the butter into smaller pieces. This is most easily done in a food-processor with a few short pulses, but can be done by hand with a round-bladed knife and a slicing action across the bowl. You only want to break up the butter into multiple smallish chunks, roughly the size of a sugar cube.

2. Next add the milk, water and egg mixture and stir everything together briefly. Cover the bowl with clingfilm and leave it in the fridge for several hours, or preferably overnight.

3. Next, tip the contents of the bowl onto a floured surface and bring it together into a square of dough. With a well-floured rolling pin, **roll** the dough out to a large square about 5mm thick. At first this will be difficult, as the dough will be very broken and lumpy. *Continued*

Needs a little skill

HANDS-ON TIME:
1 hour

HANDS-OFF TIME:
Several hours,
or overnight

BAKING TIME:
20 minutes

MAKES:
6 pains au chocolat

SPECIAL EQUIPMENT:
1 baking sheet, food-processor (optional)

STORAGE:
Best eaten on the day you bake them, or refresh them in the oven the following day

4. Once you have achieved a large square, fold one third of the square into the centre and the opposite third over that, so that you have a long rectangle. Then roll this out to the largest square you can manage, rotate it to the right by 90 degrees and fold it again in the same way. Repeat the folding, rotating and rolling four times in total, finishing by folding again so you have a neat squat rectangle. Wrap the dough in clingfilm to rest in the fridge for at least 1 hour.

5. To make the pains au chocolat, roll the dough out again on your floured surface to a roughly 40cm square. Prepare a large baking sheet by lining it with baking paper. Cut the dough in two vertically and three horizontally to make six equal rectangles.

6. Place one sixth of your 100g chocolate down the centre of each horizontal rectangle. If you have a bar of chocolate you can cut a narrow bar; if you have chips or chunks fashion a line of chocolate down the centre. Then fold each pain au chocolat so that the two sides of each rectangle cover the chocolate and overlap a little.

7. Place each pain au chocolat, seam side down, on the lined baking sheet. Then leave the baking sheet in a warm place for 2–3 hours to allow the pains au chocolat to rise.

8 Preheat the oven to 180°C (160°C fan), 350°F, Gas 4. When the pastries are visibly larger (by about 25–30 per cent), brush them with the beaten egg and bake for 20 minutes, until they are well-risen and golden brown. Take the pains au chocolat out of the oven and place on a wire rack to cool. They can be kept in an airtight container once completely cool and then warmed through in the oven for a couple of minutes.

Chocolate and Praline Roulade with Dark Chocolate Sauce

Rich dark chocolate roulade is a special dessert to have in your repertoire. This consists of a rolled flourless chocolate sponge filled with the wonderful flavour of home-made almond praline.

For the sponge
170g 70–75 per cent dark chocolate (Piura would work well)
60ml water
5 medium eggs, at room temperature, separated
170g caster sugar

For the praline cream
150g almonds
75ml water
100g caster sugar
300ml double cream, well chilled

For the dark chocolate sauce
150g dark chocolate (use the same as for the sponge)
150ml double cream
1 tablespoon caster sugar
25g unsalted butter
50–100ml milk

icing sugar, for dusting

HANDS-ON TIME:
1 hour 5 minutes

BAKING TIME:
12–15 minutes

SERVES:
8

SPECIAL EQUIPMENT:
23 × 33cm Swiss roll tin, food-processor

METHOD USED:
Melting chocolate, page 24

STORAGE:
Keep for up to 2 days in the fridge

1. To make the sponge, preheat the oven to 180°C (160°C fan), 350°F, Gas 4. Grease and **line** your Swiss roll tin.

2. **Melt** the chocolate in a bain-marie. Break the chocolate into pieces and place in a heatproof bowl with the water, set over a pan of gently simmering water, making sure that the bottom of the bowl doesn't touch the water (or use a microwave). Stir gently and when melted set to one side for a moment. Beat the egg yolks with the sugar until they are pale and aerated. In a separate large, clean bowl **whisk** the egg whites until they are firm. Then loosen the melted chocolate with some of the egg yolk mixture, before adding all the chocolate to the yolks and folding it in fully. Next loosen the chocolate and egg yolk mixture with a large spoonful of the egg whites. Carefully **fold** in all the chocolate mixture into the egg whites.

3. Pour the sponge mixture into your prepared tin, ensuring that it reaches into all corners and is an even thickness. Bake the sponge in the oven for 12–15 minutes, until a skewer comes out clean.

4. When you take your sponge out of the oven, using the baking paper, carefully slide it onto a wire rack. Next, take a clean tea towel and wet it, before wringing it out so that it is only slightly damp. Cover the top of the sponge with it – roulades have a tendency to crack when they are rolled up so doing this will keep the sponge moist as it cools and help prevent this.
Continued

5. To start the filling, **make the praline**. Put a baking sheet or tin near the stove ready to pour the praline onto when cooked. Place the 150g almonds, 75ml water and 100g sugar in a small pan over a high heat until they are boiling, stirring continuously with a wooden or heatproof spatula, so as not to burn. Continue to stir as the water boils off and the mixture becomes dry and sandy. Keep stirring, being careful not to let any one part of the contents of the pan catch as the sugar then melts, turns golden brown, and coats the nuts. As soon as all the sugar has caramelised and you have a nice even colour, take the pan off the heat and pour the nuts onto your waiting cold baking sheet. Leave the praline to one side to cool.

6. When the praline is fully cold, weigh out 150g of the caramelised nuts (reserving a few to decorate the roulade at the end) and process them to a fine powder in a food-processor. Next whip the 300ml cream to soft peaks before folding through the praline powder.

7. To make the chocolate sauce, **melt** the 150g dark chocolate with the 150ml double cream and the 1 tablespoon of caster sugar in a heatproof bowl set over a pan of gently simmering water, making sure the bottom of the bowl doesn't touch the water. Stir them while melting until they are smoothly mixed together. Remove from the heat, dot the 25g unsalted butter over the melted chocolate mixture and then beat it in. Lastly, add 50–100ml milk, depending on how thick you want your sauce, whisking it vigorously into the sauce to bring it all together. The sauce will get thicker as it cools.

8. When you are ready to assemble the roulade, remove the tea towel from the top of the sponge and gently dot and spread the praline cream over the surface, being careful not to break up the cake as you go.

9. Starting from one of the shorter ends, and using the baking paper to help you, lift and roll the sponge into a long sausage shape. Finish by carefully lifting the rolled cake onto a serving dish. Dust the roulade with icing sugar and scatter over the reserved pieces of praline (chop any larger pieces). Place the jug of sauce alongside.

Try Something Different

To make a simpler nut-free version, leave out the praline and whip the cream with a few tablespoons of sugar instead. Add a little brandy to the cream if you want to make an adult version.

Baked Chocolate
Tarts in Chocolate
Pastry with
Caramel Sauce

These tarts give the double treat of a brownie-like chocolate filling inside chocolate pastry. A sweet pastry, here enriched with cocoa powder, is a great opportunity to practise rolling pastry and filling individual tart tins.

Needs a little skill

HANDS-ON TIME:
45 minutes

HANDS-OFF TIME:
30 minutes chilling

BAKING TIME:
35 minutes

MAKES:
8 tarts

SPECIAL EQUIPMENT:
8 round 11cm individual loose-bottomed tart tins, 2cm deep

METHOD USED:
Melting chocolate, page 24

STORAGE:
Keep for up to 5 days in the fridge

For the chocolate pastry
125g unsalted butter, at room temperature
100g icing sugar
200g plain flour
25g cocoa powder
pinch of salt
2 medium egg yolks
2 tablespoons cold milk

For the filling
125g unsalted butter
200g 65 per cent dark chocolate
4 medium eggs, at room temperature
150g caster sugar
4 tablespoons plain flour
pinch of salt

For the caramel sauce
100g unsalted butter
50g caster sugar
50g golden syrup
¼ teaspoon fine salt
150ml double cream
400g crème fraîche

1. To **make the chocolate pastry**, cut the butter into several pieces and put it, along with the icing sugar, into a large bowl. Cream the butter and sugar until they are fully blended. Add the flour, cocoa powder and salt, and either rub in with your fingertips or cut in briefly, using two round-bladed knives in a crossing action, until the mixture looks like fine breadcrumbs. Next whisk the yolks and milk together, before adding to the bowl. Cut in just until the mixture starts to stick together, and you feel that the dough would come together if pressed. (Or you can make the pastry in a food-processor.)

2. Turn the dough out onto a lightly floured surface, and bring it together with floured hands with as little handling as possible. Shape the dough into a flat disc, wrap it in clingfilm and chill in the fridge for at least 30 minutes.

3. **Roll** the pastry out on a lightly floured surface so it is the thickness of a £1 coin. Keep the surface and rolling pin floured, and keep the dough moving to ensure it doesn't stick. Cut out eight 14cm circles, using a small plate as a cutting guide. Gather and re-roll the pastry trimmings so you can cut out enough pastry circles. Use them to **line** the tart tins, easing the pastry into the corners. Trim the pastry edges (wrap and keep the excess for patching up any cracks) and press the pastry into the flutes of each tin. Lightly prick the bases with a fork.
Continued

4. Place the raw tart cases into your freezer to chill completely, for at least 30 minutes, or until you are ready to make your tarts. If you are making your pastry well in advance wrap the tart cases in foil or an airtight bag and keep for up to three months.

5. When you are ready to make your tarts, preheat the oven to 190°C (170°C fan), 375°F, Gas 5. Line each pastry case with small circles of baking paper and fill with baking beans or uncooked rice. **Blind bake** for 10 minutes, remove the paper and beans and bake for a further 5 minutes, or until the base of the pastry feels sandy and there are no visible damp patches. Remove from the oven and then turn the oven down to 160°C (140°C fan), 325°F, Gas 3.

6. While the cases are baking, you can prepare the filling. **Melt** the 125g butter and 200g dark chocolate together over a very low heat in a small pan. In a large bowl whisk the 4 eggs and 150g sugar together until they are light and fluffy. Then whisk in the melted chocolate mixture. Finally **fold in** the 4 tablespoons of flour and pinch of salt, until they are fully mixed in.

7. Pour the chocolate filling into the baked pastry cases and bake on the middle shelf of the oven for 20 minutes.

8. When you take the tarts out of the oven they will be puffed up and the tops cracked but they will settle as they cool. Allow the tarts to cool completely while you make the caramel sauce.

9. Put the 100g butter, 50g sugar and 50g golden syrup in a small pan over a medium heat and stir a couple of times until they are all melted and mixed together. Bring the contents of the pan to the boil and let bubble for 5 minutes, until darkened in colour. Then, off the heat, add the ¼ teaspoon of salt and 150ml double cream, stirring continuously until everything is smoothly mixed together. Pour the sauce into a jug to let it cool.

10. When you are ready to serve the tarts, **remove from the tins.** You can either swirl the caramel sauce through the 400g crème fraîche and serve alongside the tarts in a bowl, or serve each tart with a spoonful of crème fraîche and the caramel sauce drizzled over the top.

Macarons with Cardamom Ganache

A must-have item in every French patisserie, macarons frequently feature a chocolate ganache filling. In this version a chocolate macaron shell is given a flavour punch with a spice-infused centre.

Needs a little skill

HANDS-ON TIME:
1 hour

HANDS-OFF TIME:
At least 1 hour resting

BAKING TIME:
12–13 minutes

MAKES:
30 filled macarons

METHOD USED:
Chocolate ganache, page 26

SPECIAL EQUIPMENT:
2 baking sheets, 2 piping bags, 1cm plain round piping nozzle

STORAGE:
These are best eaten the day after you make them, as the filling has had time to infuse the shell with its flavour

For the macaron shells
175g icing sugar
10g cocoa powder
100g ground almonds
100g egg whites (roughly the whites of 3 medium eggs, but do weigh them), at room temperature
45g caster sugar

For the ganache filling
25 cardamom pods
300ml double cream
300g 70 per cent dark chocolate (Grenadan or West African would work well)

1. Preheat the oven to 180°C (160°C fan), 350°F, Gas 4. Take two large sheets of baking paper and, using a cookie cutter or similar, draw rows of 3.5cm circles in pencil on one side. Try to keep the circles in neat rows and make sure they are spaced a few centimetres apart. Turn the papers over and place each one on a large flat baking sheet. If you turn the paper over you will still be able to see the circles from the other side. These are for you to use as templates in which to pipe your macaron shells.

2. To make the shells, sift the icing sugar and cocoa powder together, then stir in the ground almonds. In a separate bowl, **whisk** the egg whites until they are foamy, then add half the caster sugar and continue whisking. When the egg whites are firm add the remaining caster sugar and whisk it in until the mixture is thick and glossy. Add the dry ingredients to the egg whites and **fold** them through carefully and thoroughly. This is called the 'macaronade'.

3. Spoon the macaronade into a large piping bag fitted with the 1cm plain nozzle. Then **pipe** even-sized macarons onto your lined baking sheets, using the circles as a guide.

Continued

4. Go over the piped macarons with a damp finger to gently press down any little peaks left from piping the mixture. Leave the baking sheets to one side for at least an hour before baking – you can leave them overnight if needed. This allows the macarons to develop a skin, which prevents them rising with a crack in the top and encourages them to create a 'foot', which is characteristic of the way finished macarons should look.

5. Bake the shells for 12–13 minutes until they are well risen, crisp and have well-defined 'feet'. Allow them to cool completely before removing them from the baking sheets.

6. To make the **ganache** filling, crush the 25 cardamom pods in a pestle and mortar to reveal the seeds inside. Add to a small pan with the 300ml double cream and place over a low-medium heat to heat through without boiling. Take it off the heat and then leave it to infuse for half an hour.

7. Break the 300g dark chocolate into small pieces so that it has the best chance to melt evenly and place in a heatproof bowl. Heat the cream back up until it is just steaming, then pour the cream through a strainer onto the chocolate. Stir the hot cream through the chocolate, gradually stirring the chocolate as it melts, to create your ganache.

8. When both the ganache and the macaron shells are cool, sort the shells into pairs. Put the ganache into a piping bag – a disposable one will do fine for this, with the end snipped off. Then pipe some ganache onto one half of each pair of shells, top them with the second half and twist the two to spread the ganache evenly and sandwich the shells together. Repeat until you have used up all your shells.

Try Something Different

You can flavour the ganache with other herbs or spices instead of cardamom. Try infusing the cream with ½ chopped fresh red chilli, the grated zest of 1 orange or a handful of fresh mint leaves.

White Chocolate Easter Egg and Moulded Chocolates

The secret to making chocolate Easter eggs and shapes that will last is to ensure the chocolate is properly **tempered**. However if you know you are going to eat the chocolate shapes straight away, and just want to have some fun with the moulds, have a go at making the shapes by just melting the chocolate and using that instead. Chocolate moulds come in every possible shape and size. You'll need to temper at least 300g of chocolate as it is difficult to work with smaller amounts – this will give you enough to make one large hollow Easter egg and several small chocolates.

Needs a little skill

HANDS-ON TIME:
1 hour

HANDS-OFF TIME:
30 minutes to
1 hour setting

MAKES:
1 large Easter egg
and several small
chocolates

SPECIAL EQUIPMENT:
Chocolate
moulds, kitchen
thermometer, palette
knife or scraper

METHOD USED:
Melting chocolate,
page 24
Tempering
chocolate, page 29

STORAGE:
Tempered chocolate
will keep for several
months in a cool
place in an airtight
container

To fill the moulds
300g white chocolate
300g dark chocolate

To decorate
About 50g contrasting chocolate
(optional)

Sweets or small chocolates to fill the egg (optional)

1. Before you start to fill your moulds you can decorate them. Firstly, ensure that they are spotlessly clean, as anything on their surface will come off on your finished chocolates. The high shine on the chocolates made by top patissiers comes from the mirror-like surface of the insides of their moulds. **Melt** a small amount of contrasting chocolate in a heatproof bowl set over a pan of gently simmering water, and then paint or **pipe** that carefully into a pattern on the inside of the moulds. Allow any pattern you create to set fully before you fill the moulds with your chocolate.

Continued

2. To **temper** your white chocolate, place 210g of it in a heatproof bowl set over a pan of barely simmering water. Using your kitchen thermometer, measure the temperature of the chocolate as it melts. Stir it to ensure the heat is evenly distributed and do not allow it to get above 40–45°C (104–113°F).

3. Just before it reaches temperature (as it is likely to continue to rise for a little while after you remove the heat source), take the bowl off the heat, and continue to stir to melt any visible pieces of chocolate. Then add in the remaining 90g chocolate and stir this into the melted chocolate. Keep stirring, as the newly added chocolate melts and the temperature comes down. Keep checking the temperature of the chocolate; you want it to reach 27°C (80.6°F).

4. When it has come down to the correct temperature, place the bowl back over the simmering water very briefly, keeping a watchful eye on the temperature. You want it to come back up to 30°C (86°F), but no higher. Bear in mind that the temperature will rise quickly, and continue to rise once you have removed the heat source.

5. When the white chocolate is at 30°C (86°F) leave the bowl off the heat, dip a knife into the molten chocolate and scrape off one side on the edge of the bowl. Allow the remaining chocolate on the knife to set to test if it has been successfully tempered. Pop the knife in the fridge to allow the remaining chocolate on the knife to set. Touch the set chocolate very lightly – if it feels smooth and dry and doesn't take the impression of your fingertip then it is tempered.

6. If you just want to melt the chocolate without tempering, place the 300g chocolate in a heatproof bowl set over a pan of gently simmering water, making sure the bottom of the bowl doesn't touch the water.

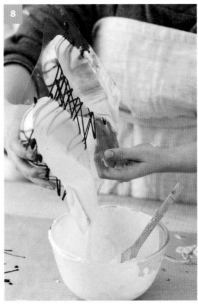

7. When you have a bowl of melted or tempered chocolate you need to work quickly, as the longer you take the thicker the chocolate will become as it cools. To fill a hollow Easter egg mould, fill the mould with enough chocolate to fill to the brim.

8. Wait for a moment, and then turn the mould upside down over your bowl of molten chocolate and allow all but a fine coating of chocolate to pour back out. Repeat to make the second half. Then scrape the surface of the mould clean with a palette knife or scraper. Use the leftover chocolate to fill your individual moulds.

To make individual chocolates

9. To fill small moulds to create solid chocolates, fill the moulds with tempered or melted chocolate until they are full and use a palette knife or scraper to scrape off any surface chocolate and give the chocolates a flat underside.

10. Set all the filled moulds in a cool place to allow the chocolate to harden. This should take up to 30 minutes for a hollow shell; solid chocolates may take up to 1 hour. Then turn the moulded chocolates out onto clean baking paper. Tempered chocolates in stiff moulds will just pop out if you tap them upside down – you can twist them a little like ice-cube trays if they are resistant. Silicone moulds can be peeled off.

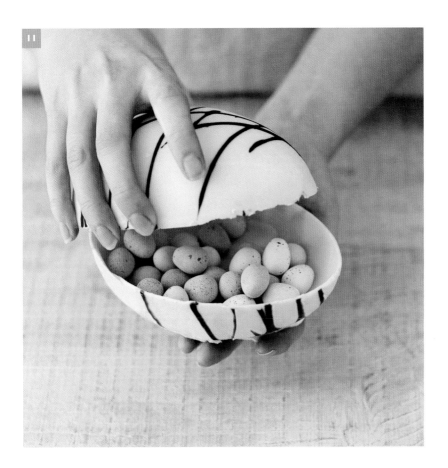

11. If you want you can fill your hollow Easter egg with sweets or small chocolates. Place a few sweets in one chocolate egg half. Press the other half onto the base of a hot pan for a few seconds before holding both halves together. Allow to set fully.

Try Something Different

You can use any chocolate to fill your moulds but different chocolates have different tempering temperatures, so if you don't use white chocolate, do refer to the section on tempering, page 29. When filling moulds to create solid chocolates you could use both white and dark or milk chocolate and swirl them together to make two-tone chocolates.

Hazelnut Dacquoise with Dark Chocolate and Praline

In this dacquoise the classic flavour combination of dark chocolate and hazelnuts is taken to another level. A simple hazelnut meringue is layered with chocolate cream and chocolate ganache, then topped with irresistible caramelised hazelnuts.

Up for a challenge

HANDS-ON TIME:
1½ hours

BAKING TIME:
30–35 minutes

SERVES:
12–16

SPECIAL EQUIPMENT:
2 baking sheets, each 25 × 35cm

METHOD USED:
Chocolate ganache, page 26
Melting chocolate, page 24

STORAGE:
Keep in the fridge for up to 2 days

For the hazelnut dacquoise
400g hazelnuts, lightly roasted
275g caster sugar
8 medium egg whites, at room temperature
butter, for greasing

For the praline
150g hazelnuts
75ml water
100g caster sugar

For the ganache
300ml double cream
50g caster sugar
200g 65 per cent dark chocolate

For the chocolate cream
100g 65 per cent dark chocolate
50g golden syrup
300ml double cream

To make the hazelnut dacquoise

1. Preheat the oven to 160°C (140°C fan), 325°F, Gas 3 and line the two rectangular baking sheets with baking paper and then lightly **butter** the paper.

2. Grind the hazelnuts with 175g of the sugar in a food-processor until the nuts are very finely ground. Then in a separate clean bowl, **whisk** the egg whites until they are white and frothy. Add the remaining 100g sugar a little at a time as you continue to whisk the whites until they are smooth, glossy and stiff. Next, add the ground hazelnuts and sugar to the egg whites and **fold** them through until they are fully incorporated.

3. Divide the meringue mixture between the two prepared baking sheets; spread almost up to the edges of the baking sheets to form two rectangles that are the same size, making sure they form an even layer. Bake the meringues for 30–35 minutes, until they are lightly golden. Cover two wire racks with baking paper, to prevent sticking, and then turn them out to cool.
Continued

To make the praline

4. Put a baking sheet or tin near the stove ready to pour the **praline** onto when cooked. Then place the 150g hazelnuts, 75ml water and 100g sugar in a small pan over a high heat until they are boiling, stirring continuously with a wooden or heatproof spatula, so as not to burn. Continue to stir as the water boils off and the mixture becomes dry and sandy. Keep stirring, being careful not to let any one part of the contents of the pan catch, as the sugar melts, then turns golden brown, and coats the nuts. As soon as all the sugar has caramelised and you have a nice even colour, take the pan off the heat and pour the nuts onto your waiting cold baking sheet. Try to separate the nuts out as far as possible while they are still hot and malleable, so you have some nicely separate nuts to decorate your dacquoise. This will make around twice as much praline as you need, but it is tricky to make it in smaller quantities, as the heat gets to it too fast and it is more prone to burning. You can keep what you have left in an airtight container for 2–3 weeks. (It would work well in place of the almond praline for the roulade filling on page 130.)

To make the ganache

5. Heat 250ml of the 300ml cream and the 50g sugar in a small pan until they just come to the boil. Set the cream to one side for a moment, so that it is no longer scalding hot. Put the 200g chocolate into a heatproof bowl, then pour over the warm cream, and stir it gradually and thoroughly until all the chocolate has melted and you have a smooth **ganache**. If your ganache looks like splitting at any point add the remaining 50ml cream and beat it thoroughly to bring it back to a smooth consistency. Then set it to one side to cool and firm up a little.

To make the chocolate cream

6. Melt the 100g of chocolate and 50g syrup together in a small pan or the microwave. Then whip the 300ml double cream until it is thick and just starting to hold its shape (don't over-whip it or you may end up making butter). Use a spoonful or two of the cream to loosen the chocolate mixture, then **fold** it all through the whipped cream until you have a smooth chocolate cream.

To assemble the dacquoise

7. When the meringues are cold, turn them out onto a large board and gently remove the baking paper. With a bread knife, cutting carefully with a gentle sawing action so as not to tear them, trim the ends to neaten and then slice each in half widthways so you have four equal rectangles.

8. Place one rectangle of meringue onto a serving plate or cake board. Spoon half the chocolate cream on to it, and spread it out to cover evenly.

9. Place the second layer of meringue on top and cover that with half the cooled ganache. Next place the third layer of meringue on top, before spreading that with the remaining chocolate cream. The fourth rectangle placed on top forms the top of the cake, covered in the remaining half of the ganache.

10. To decorate the top layer, break up the praline into individual caramelised nuts, and then chop enough of them roughly to scatter across the ganache topping. Keep the cake in the fridge until you are ready to serve.

Bûche de Noël

A festive centrepiece, this cake deliciously combines a rolled cocoa sponge, spiced buttercream and dark chocolate ganache, decorated with white chocolate **ganache** snowballs and gilded chocolate leaves. Use non-toxic leaves (don't use Ivy) that are robust enough to be painted, but thin enough that they can be peeled off the chocolate once it is set. The buttercream flavouring is inspired by the classic Belgian 'speculoos' biscuit.

*Up for
a challenge*

HANDS-ON TIME:
2½ hours

BAKING TIME:
15 minutes

MAKES:
16 slices

**SPECIAL
EQUIPMENT:**
25 × 35cm Swiss
roll tin, kitchen
thermometer, pastry
brush, fresh leaves

METHOD USED:
Chocolate ganache,
page 26
Tempering
chocolate, page 29

STORAGE:
Keep for 3–4 days in
a cool place or the
fridge in an airtight
container

For the chocolate sponge
6 medium eggs, at room temperature, separated
130g caster sugar
60g cocoa powder, sifted
pinch of salt
icing sugar, for dusting

For the 'speculoos' buttercream
3 teaspoons ground cinnamon
½ teaspoon ground ginger
¼ teaspoon ground cloves
¼ nutmeg, grated
¼ teaspoon ground cardamom
freshly ground black pepper, to taste
125g unsalted butter, softened
300g icing sugar
1 tablespoon milk

For the ganache covering
250g 60–65 per cent dark chocolate (Grenadan would work well)
300ml double cream
25g unsalted butter, in small pieces

For the white chocolate snowball decorations
150ml double cream
125g white chocolate, broken into pieces
25g unsalted butter, in small pieces
icing sugar, for dusting

For the white chocolate leaves
300g white chocolate
edible gold dust or glitter

To make the decorations
1. You may like to make the decorations first, so they are ready and waiting when you finish the cake. They can all be made in advance and kept until you are ready to use them. The chocolate leaves could be used to decorate any celebration cake, such as the Three Colours Chocolate Cake on page 168.

2. For the white chocolate snowballs make a **ganache** by heating the cream to just below boiling point and pouring it over the white chocolate in a heatproof bowl, stirring to melt the chocolate. When all is amalgamated add the butter and stir that in as well. Then leave the ganache to set in the fridge for at least 1 hour.
Continued

3. Roll spoonfuls of the cold ganache between your palms, working quickly and using icing sugar to dust your hands to prevent too much sticking. Roll each finished ball in plenty of icing sugar to make a snowball. If you feel ambitious you could even create a snowman. Keep your finished snowballs in an airtight container in the fridge until you are ready to use them, or for up to 2 weeks.

4. To make the chocolate leaves, **temper** some white chocolate. It is difficult to temper chocolate using much less than 300g. This is more than you need for this recipe, so you may want to make the decorations when you are tempering chocolate for something else as well. The decorations will then keep in a cool place in an airtight container for several months.

5. Place 210g of the 300g chocolate in a heatproof bowl set over a pan of gently simmering water. Using your kitchen thermometer, measure the temperature of the chocolate as it melts. Stir it to ensure the heat is evenly distributed and do not allow it to get above 40–45°C (104–113°F). Just before it reaches temperature (it is likely to continue to rise for a little while after you remove the heat source), take the bowl off the heat, and continue to stir to melt any visible pieces of chocolate. Then add the remaining 90g of chocolate and stir this into the melted chocolate. Keep stirring, as the newly added chocolate melts and the temperature comes down. Keep checking the temperature of the chocolate; you want it to reach 27°C (80.6°F). When it has come down to the correct temperature, place the bowl back over the simmering water very briefly, keeping a watchful eye on the temperature. You want it to come back up to 30°C (86°F), but no higher. Bear in mind that the temperature will rise quickly, and continue to rise once you have removed the heat source.

6. When the white chocolate is at 30°C (86°F) leave the bowl off the heat and dip a knife into the molten chocolate to test if it has been successfully tempered. Pop the knife in the fridge to allow the remaining chocolate on the knife to set. Touch the set chocolate very lightly – if it feels smooth and dry and doesn't take the impression of your fingertip then it is tempered. Assemble your real leaves from the garden (making sure they are clean and dry), ready to create chocolate ones.

7. When you have a bowl of tempered chocolate work quickly, as the longer you take, the thicker the chocolate will become as it cools. Paint some of the tempered chocolate onto your leaves and allow the chocolate to set fully.

8. Carefully peel off the fresh leaves to reveal your chocolate ones. Brush the chocolate leaves with edible gold dust or glitter for a Christmassy effect.

To make the chocolate sponge
9. Preheat the oven to 180°C (160°C fan), 350°F, Gas 4. Grease and **line** the Swiss roll tin with baking paper. Whisk the 6 egg yolks and 130g sugar vigorously until they have thickened and are light in colour. Add the 60g cocoa powder and pinch of salt to the egg yolk mixture and **fold** it in with a large spatula. In a separate clean bowl, **whisk** the egg whites to stiff peaks (this will take about 2 minutes by hand using a rotary whisk). Loosen the cocoa mixture by stirring in a large dollop of the egg whites, before adding the remaining egg whites and then **fold** them in, just until there are no more visible patches of egg white.

10. Pour the cake batter into the prepared Swiss roll tin and bake it for 15 minutes. While it is in the oven lay out a sheet of baking paper larger than the cake tin and dust it all over with icing sugar. This will prevent the cake from sticking when you roll it later. Remove from the oven and as soon as you are able to handle the sponge, turn it upside down on your prepared baking paper.
Continued

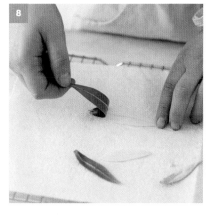

11. Gently peel off the baking paper it was baked in, and then starting from one of the shorter sides, use your hands and the baking paper underneath the sponge to lift it, and roll it up into a tight sausage. Rolling the sponge before it cools means that when you are ready to fill it, when the cake is cold, it will have that shape already and be easy to re-roll without cracking.

To make the 'speculoos' buttercream
12. To make the buttercream, first make the speculoos spice mix. Combine the 3 teaspoons of ground cinnamon, ½ teaspoon of ground ginger, ¼ teaspoon of ground cloves, ¼ grated nutmeg, ¼ teaspoon of ground cardamom and a twist or two of black pepper and mix them together in a small pot or jar. You will not need all of the mix for this one

recipe, but you can keep the rest for another cake.

13. Place the 125g butter and 3 teaspoons of the spice mix (or to taste) in a bowl with the 300g icing sugar and mash together with a fork. Add the tablespoon of milk and continue to work the icing ingredients together until you have a smooth icing.

To make the ganache covering
14. For the ganache, place the 250g chocolate in a heatproof bowl, then heat the 300ml cream to just below boiling point. Pour the hot cream over the chocolate and stir gently to make a ganache. When the chocolate is fully melted and amalgamated add the 25g butter and stir that in too.

To assemble and decorate

15. When the cake is cold and the ganache has firmed up you can assemble your cake. Unroll the sponge and spread the buttercream filling over what will be the inside surface, before rolling the cake up again as tightly as you can. Then place the cake onto your serving dish. To create the effect of branches, cut off one end of the roll at an angle and place the off-cut with the cut end positioned against the side of the roll (see picture on page 154). Then carefully use a knife or palette knife to spread the ganache over the top and sides of the cake, covering it completely.

16. Drag the prongs of a fork over the surface of the ganache to create the effect of wood bark. On the ends a skewer dragged in a spiral motion can mimic the rings inside a tree trunk. Place the cake in the fridge for about 30 minutes for the ganache to set fully while you assemble the decorations.

17. To decorate the cake dust the top with icing sugar, add chocolate leaves to the trunk of the cake and scatter snowballs on your serving plate.

Try Something Different

If you would prefer a plainer buttercream replace the spices with a teaspoon of vanilla extract.
You can make the leaves in the same way using milk or dark chocolate. Or you can make life easier by decorating with shop bought Christmas decorations or figurines.

Box of Chocolates

Now that you have mastered **tempering**, you can try the ultimate chocolate creation – a whole box of treats! All of the recipes here will make bigger quantities than you will need for one box of chocolates, but they are fiddly to make in smaller quantities. You could either make them all and make lots of boxes with different selections in each to give as gifts, or choose your favourites

and just make those. It makes sense to prepare all the fillings in advance, so that you can then temper the chocolate and **enrobe** and finish the chocolates in one go. This is possible for all the recipes here, except the cinnamon-filled chocolates, as the shells need to be created, filled and then topped off in three different stages, so you will need to temper chocolate twice.

Up for a challenge

HANDS-ON TIME:
4–5 hours

BAKING TIME:
10–12 minutes

MAKES:
15 caramels; 70–80 sablé biscuits; 15–20 brandy truffles; 15 Earl Grey truffles; 15–20 cinnamon-filled chocolates; 25–50 enrobed nuts; 10–15 mendiants

SPECIAL EQUIPMENT:
Kitchen thermometer, 23cm square silicone cake tin, baking sheets, 3.5cm round cutter, 20cm square cake tins to set the ganache (optional), piping bag and 5mm plain round nozzle, chocolate moulds

METHOD USED:
Chocolate ganache, page 26; Tempering chocolate, page 29; Enrobing chocolate, page 32

STORAGE:
Ganache and caramel will keep for up to 2 weeks, mendiants and enrobed nuts for up to 1 month, sablés for 4–5 days, all in a cool place in airtight containers.

For the caramels
75ml whipping cream
½ teaspoon sea salt
½ teaspoon vanilla extract
20g liquid glucose
150g caster sugar
75g unsalted butter, cut into cubes

For the walnut sablé biscuits
125g unsalted butter
100g caster sugar
1 medium egg, at room temperature
125g plain flour
100g walnuts, finely ground in a food-processor
½ teaspoon salt
½ teaspoon baking powder

For the brandy truffles
150g 70 per cent dark chocolate (Grenadan or Virunga would work well)
1 tablespoon brandy
150ml double cream
25g butter, cut into small pieces

For the Earl Grey truffles
150g 60–65 per cent chocolate (Ecuadorian would be perfect)
100ml Earl Grey tea

For the cinnamon-filled chocolates
150g milk chocolate
150ml double cream
2 cinnamon sticks
25g butter, cut into small pieces

For the caramelised nuts
150g hazelnuts, almonds, macadamia nuts or peanuts
75ml water
100g caster sugar

To enrobe and for the filled chocolate shells
900g dark chocolate, or 300g each of 3 different chocolates (dark, white and milk)

For the mendiants
A handful or two of mixed nuts, roasted

To decorate
Cocoa nibs
Earl Grey tea leaves
Small amounts of contrasting chocolate

Continued

To make the caramels

1. To make the caramels, first put the 75ml cream, ½ teaspoon sea salt and ½ teaspoon vanilla into a jug ready to pour when needed. Then put the 20g glucose and a little of the 150g sugar into a heavy-based pan and heat it slowly until the sugar starts to melt. Add the remaining sugar, little by little, until all the sugar is melted. Try not to stir the caramel as it forms, but swirl the pan if needed. Keep heating the pan until you have a good conker colour. The secret to a good caramel flavour is to take it just to the point before it burns.

2. Next, add the cream, salt and vanilla mixture a little at a time, stirring it in thoroughly. The sugar will bubble fiercely when it comes into contact with the cold cream, but keep adding and stirring it in. Using your kitchen thermometer test the temperature of the mixture. When it is 110°C (230°F) you can add the 75g butter, bit by bit, stirring until it is all incorporated. Then heat the mixture to 125°C (257°F), before pouring it into a 23cm square silicone cake tin. Store it in a cool dry place until cold and firm, before cutting the caramel into squares or rectangles, ready for enrobing.

To make the walnut sablé biscuits

3. To make the sablé biscuits, cream the 125g butter and 100g sugar together until light and fluffy. Then beat in the egg. Combine the 125g flour, 100g ground walnuts, ½ teaspoon of salt and ½ teaspoon of baking powder in another bowl, then **fold** them into the butter mixture. Mix this together just enough to bring it together into dough. You will

need floured hands to do this, as it is a very soft dough. Wrap the dough in clingfilm and rest in the fridge for 1 hour.

4. Preheat the oven to 180°C (160°C fan), 350°F, Gas 4 and line two baking sheets with baking paper. **Roll** the dough out on a floured surface to a thickness of about 5mm. Use the 3.5cm round cutter to **cut out** your shapes and place them a little apart on the lined baking sheets. You will need to flour your rolling pin and cutter well to prevent the dough from sticking.

5. Bake the biscuits for around 10–12 minutes, until they are lightly golden. Allow them to cool on the baking sheets for a minute, then **lift** them to a wire rack to cool completely, ready for enrobing.

To make the brandy truffle filling
6. To make the brandy truffle filling, break the 150g chocolate into small pieces and put into a bowl with the tablespoon of brandy. Put the 150ml cream in a pan and bring to just below boiling point. Pour the hot cream over the chocolate and stir to melt the chocolate, gradually incorporating all the chocolate into the cream to make a **ganache**. Add the 25g butter, a little at a time, and beat the ganache until it is all smoothly amalgamated.

7. Pour the ganache into a 20cm square cake tin lined with clingfilm, or leave in its bowl if you want to hand roll the truffles. Place the brandy ganache in the fridge to harden for about 30 minutes, then **cut or roll the ganache** into even-sized pieces.

To make the Earl Grey truffle filling
8. To make the Earl Grey truffle filling, break the 150g chocolate into small pieces and place into a bowl. Ensure that the 100ml tea is hot but not boiling, and a good clear amber colour. You don't want it tannic and over-brewed; neither do you want tea so weak that the flavour will not come through in the finished chocolates. Pour the hot tea over the chocolate and stir to melt the chocolate, gradually incorporating all the chocolate into the tea to make a ganache.

9. Pour the ganache into a 20cm square cake tin lined with clingfilm, or leave in its bowl if you want to hand roll the truffles later. Water ganaches such as this (made without cream or butter) are more delicate to handle, and you may be better off cutting it than rolling. Place the mixture in the fridge to harden for about 30 minutes, then **cut the ganache** into even-sized pieces.
Continued

To make the ganache for the cinnamon-filled chocolates

10. To make the ganache filling for the cinnamon-filled chocolates, break the 150g chocolate into small pieces and put into a bowl. Put the 150ml cream in a pan with the 2 cinnamon sticks and bring to just below boiling point. Then leave to infuse for 30 minutes, before straining and returning to the pan. Heat the cream again until it is just steaming. Then pour the hot cream over the chocolate and stir to melt, gradually incorporating all the chocolate into the cream to make a ganache. Add the 25g butter and beat into the ganache until it is all smoothly amalgamated. **Fill** a piping bag fitted with a 5mm plain round nozzle with the ganache and set to one side until you have prepared the chocolate shells.

To make the caramelised nuts

11. To make the caramelised nuts, put the 150g nuts, 75ml water and 100g sugar into a small saucepan and make a **praline**. When you pour the hot praline onto a baking sheet to cool, try and separate the nuts into individual nuts, or clusters of the size you will want to enrobe later. Don't worry too much about this as you can always break it up to the right size.

To temper the chocolate

12. To enrobe all the ganaches, nuts and sablés, and create the shells for the filled chocolates, you need to **temper** your 900g chocolate. Place 630g of your 900g of chocolate in a heatproof bowl set over a pan of simmering water. Using your kitchen thermometer, measure the temperature of the

chocolate as it melts. Stir it to ensure the heat is evenly distributed and do not allow it to get above the correct temperature (40–45°C/104–113°F for white chocolate, 45–50°C/113–122°F for dark and milk chocolate). At that top temperature, or just before as it is likely to continue to rise for a little while after you remove the heat source, take the bowl off the heat, and continue to stir to melt any visible pieces of chocolate. Then add in the remaining 270g of chocolate and stir this into the melted chocolate. Keep stirring, as the newly added chocolate melts and the temperature comes down. Keep checking the temperature of the chocolate – you want it to reach 27°C (80.6°F) for milk and white chocolate, 28–29°C (82.4–84.2°F) for dark chocolate. When it has come down to the correct temperature, place the bowl back over the simmering water very briefly, keeping a watchful eye on the temperature. You want it to come back up to working temperature (30°C/86°F for white and milk chocolate, 32°C/89°F for dark chocolate) but no higher. Bear in mind that the temperature will rise quickly, and continue to rise once you have removed the heat source.

13. When the chocolate is at working temperature leave the bowl off the heat and dip a knife into the molten chocolate to test if it has been successfully tempered while you assemble your ganaches and other fillings. Scrape off one side on the edge of the bowl and allow the remaining chocolate to set in the fridge. Touch the set chocolate very lightly; if it feels smooth and dry

and doesn't take the impression of your fingertip then it is tempered.

To make the cinnamon-filled chocolates

14. When you have a bowl of tempered chocolate, work quickly as the longer you take the thicker the chocolate will become as it cools. For the cinnamon-filled chocolates, use enough chocolate to fill the mould to the brim, wait for a moment, and then turn the mould upside down over your bowl of molten chocolate and allow all but a fine coating of chocolate to pour back out. Then scrape the surface of the mould clean with a palette knife or scraper. Set the filled mould to one side for about 30 minutes to allow the chocolate to harden.

15. When the shells are set **pipe** in the cinnamon ganache and leave to set for at least 30 minutes, before covering the whole mould with more tempered chocolate. Then scrape all the excess off, leaving a flush surface. Leave the bases to harden, before turning the filled chocolates out.

Continued

To enrobe the caramels, brandy truffles, Earl Grey truffles and caramelised nuts

16. To **enrobe** the caramels, the brandy truffles, the Earl Grey truffles and the caramelised nuts, dip them into the bowl of tempered chocolate with a fork, then pull them up, ensuring they are fully covered and allowing the excess molten chocolate to drip off. Then place them carefully on baking paper to set.

To finish the walnut sablés

17. To complete the walnut sablés, hold each biscuit between two fingers and dip the far side of the biscuit in the tempered chocolate to half-coat it. Lay the dipped sablés on baking paper to set.

To make the mendiants

18. To make the mendiants take your remaining tempered chocolate and drop circles of it onto a sheet of clean baking paper. Then, before it hardens, drop clusters of roasted nuts onto the circles. Allow them to harden into flat, nut-studded discs.

To decorate the chocolates

19. If you want to decorate your chocolates with distinguishing toppings, do so as you enrobe them. Drop a few cocoa nibs onto the brandy truffles or a couple of tea leaves onto the Earl Grey truffles before their coating is set. Or melt small amounts of contrasting chocolate and **pipe** dots, stripes or marks onto the top of each chocolate after they are set. To assemble a box of chocolates, take a few of each of your creations and place them in a display box.

Three Colours
Chocolate Cake

This centrepiece cake is a three-tier stunner. A rich chocolate mousse covers layers of dark, milk and white chocolate cake that are revealed as you cut the first slice. If you are short on time, you can make this cake without the tempered chocolate decorations.

For the dark chocolate cake
100g 65 per cent dark chocolate, broken into pieces
75g unsalted butter
150g caster sugar
125g plain flour, sifted
2 tablespoons cocoa powder, sifted
1 teaspoon baking powder
pinch of salt
75ml soured cream
150ml milk
2 medium eggs, at room temperature

For the milk chocolate cake
100g 35 per cent minimum milk chocolate, broken into pieces
75g unsalted butter
150g caster sugar
150g plain flour
1 teaspoon baking powder
pinch of salt
75ml soured cream
150ml milk
2 medium eggs, at room temperature

For the white chocolate cake
80g ground almonds
40g plain flour
pinch of salt
120g icing sugar
80g unsalted butter
100g white chocolate, broken into pieces
4 medium egg whites, at room temperature

For the chocolate mousse
300g 65 per cent dark chocolate
300g unsalted butter, cut into small pieces
6 medium eggs, separated
200g caster sugar

For the decorations
300g white, milk or dark chocolate (or use all three)

Note: This recipe uses uncooked eggs in the mousse.

HANDS-ON TIME:
2½–3½ hours, including making decorations

BAKING TIME:
1 hour 20 minutes

MAKES:
16 slices

SPECIAL EQUIPMENT:
Acetate sheets, kitchen thermometer, scraper, 3 × 23cm loose-bottomed cake tins

METHOD USED:
Tempering chocolate, page 29
Melting chocolate, page 24

STORAGE:
Keep in the fridge for up to 4 days

To make the decorations
1. First make your decorations, so they are ready when you come to make the cake. This can be done several weeks ahead if you wish. **Temper** whichever colours of chocolate you want to use; white chocolate makes the greatest contrast with the dark chocolate mousse, or use all three for something spectacular. You will find it difficult to temper an amount that is less than 300g so you may want to make the decorations when you are tempering chocolate for something else as well. Spread acetate sheets on a flat work surface.
Continued

2. To temper 300g chocolate, place 210g of it in a heatproof bowl over a pan of barely simmering water. Using your kitchen thermometer, measure the temperature of the chocolate as it melts. Stir it to ensure the heat is evenly distributed and do not allow it to get above 45–50°C (113–122°F) for dark and milk chocolate, or 40–45°C (104–113°F) for white chocolate. Take the bowl off the heat, and continue to stir to melt any remaining pieces of chocolate. Then add the remaining 90g of chocolate and stir this into the melted chocolate. Keep stirring as the newly added chocolate melts and the temperature comes down. Keep checking the temperature of the chocolate; you want it to reach 28–29°C (82.4–84.2) for dark chocolate and 27°C (80.6°F) for milk and white chocolate. When it has come down to the correct temperature, place the bowl back over the simmering water very briefly, keeping a watchful eye on the temperature. You want it to come back up to 32°C (89°F) for dark chocolate and 30°C (86°F) for milk and white chocolate, but no higher. Bear in mind that the temperature will rise quickly, and continue to rise once you have removed the bowl from the heat source.

3. Dip a knife into the molten chocolate to test if it has been successfully tempered. Scrape off one side on the edge of the bowl and allow the remaining chocolate to set in the fridge. Touch the set chocolate very lightly; if it feels smooth and dry and doesn't take the impression of your fingertip then it is tempered. When each chocolate is at its optimum working temperature spread a thin layer onto your acetate sheet, using a palette knife or scraper. Try and do this in a simple stroke or two, so as not to overwork the chocolate. Then clean your scraper and wait for the chocolate to firm up a little.

4. When the chocolate is only just still malleable, press into the chocolate with the scraper and push it along, forming chocolate ruffles as it lifts away from the acetate. Allow the decorations to harden fully and then keep the finished decorations in an airtight container in a cool place until you are ready to make the cake.

To make the cakes
5. When you are ready to start baking, preheat your oven to 180°C (160°C fan), 350°F, Gas 4. Grease and **line** the bases of the three cake tins.

6. To make the dark chocolate cake, **melt** the 100g chocolate in a heatproof bowl set over a pan of gently simmering water, making sure the bottom of the bowl doesn't touch the water (or use a microwave), and set it to one side for a minute. Then cream the 75g butter and 150g sugar together until light and fluffy. Mix the 125g flour, 2 tablespoons of cocoa powder, 1 teaspoon of baking powder and pinch of salt together in a separate bowl. Whisk the 75ml soured cream and 150ml milk together in another separate bowl or jug. Then add the 2 eggs, one at a time, to the butter and sugar, beating well after each addition. Next, beat the melted chocolate into the butter and egg mixture. Then add the flour and milk mixtures to the chocolate, butter and eggs. Do this bit by bit, alternating between the two, until you are left with a smooth cake batter. Pour the batter into one of the prepared tins, and bake the cake for 25–30 minutes. The cake is done when the top springs back when pressed and a skewer comes out clean. Leave it to cool slightly before turning out of its tin onto a wire rack.

7. While the dark chocolate cake is baking you can get on with making the milk chocolate cake. Melt the 100g milk chocolate as above and set it to one side for a minute. Cream the 75g butter and 150g sugar together until light, and mix the 150g flour, pinch of salt and teaspoon of baking powder together in a separate bowl. Whisk the 75ml soured cream and 150ml milk together in a separate bowl or jug. Then add the 2 eggs, one at a time, to the butter and sugar, beating well after each addition. Then beat the melted chocolate into the butter and egg mixture. Next add the flour and milk mixtures, a little at a time, alternating between the two, as above, until you are left with a smooth cake batter. Pour the batter into one of the prepared tins, and bake for 25–30 minutes. When the cake is done leave it to cool slightly, before turning out of its tin onto a wire rack.

Continued

8. To make the white chocolate cake put the 80g ground almonds, 40g flour, pinch of salt and 120g icing sugar into a large bowl. Melt the 80g butter and 100g white chocolate together in the microwave or in a heatproof bowl set over a pan of barely simmering water, before pouring them over the dry ingredients. Whisk the 4 egg whites lightly until they are slightly frothy and add them to the bowl. Beat everything together until you have a smooth mixture, then pour it into your final cake tin and bake for 20 minutes. Allow the cake to cool a little in its tin before turning it out onto a wire rack to cool completely.

To make the chocolate mousse
9. To make the mousse, melt the 300g dark chocolate with the 300g butter in a small pan over a low heat, stirring occasionally until they are well combined. In a separate bowl beat the 6 egg yolks together with the 200g sugar until they are smooth and the sugar has dissolved. Add the chocolate and butter to the egg yolk mixture and stir them together. In a separate bowl, **whisk** the egg whites to stiff peaks and then carefully **fold** in to the chocolate mixture until there are no more visible patches of egg white. Place the mousse in the fridge for at least an hour to firm up.

To assemble the cake

10. To assemble the cake, place the dark chocolate cake layer onto a plate or stand, then scoop a large spoonful of the chocolate mousse on top, making sure to leave enough to fill between all three cakes and cover the top and sides. Spread the mousse in an even layer with a large knife or palette knife. Then top with the milk chocolate cake and another layer of mousse.

11. Put the white chocolate cake on top as the third and final layer, before spreading the remaining mousse to cover the top and sides of the cake. If your kitchen is warm you may like to put the cake in the fridge to cool a little before finally smoothing down of the mousse and topping with your chocolate ruffles. Keep the cake in the fridge, but take it out of the fridge to come closer to room temperature before serving.

Try Something Different

For a simpler version of this showstopper you could make it with three layers of just one type of chocolate cake. To decorate you could simply grate a contrasting layer of white chocolate over the dark chocolate mousse.

A Walk in the Black Forest

This spectacular plated dessert takes inspiration from the classic flavour combinations of Black Forest Gateau. Dark chocolate torte and white chocolate ice cream are accompanied by cherry compote and topped off with a white chocolate shard.

For the ice cream
6 medium egg yolks
600ml whipping cream
250g white chocolate, in chips or chopped
3 tablespoons kirsch

For the pecan nut torte
200g unsalted butter
200g 60–65 per cent dark chocolate (Ecuadorian would be a good choice)
5 medium eggs, at room temperature
200g caster sugar

150g pecan nuts, ground to a fine powder
pinch of salt

For the cherry compote
500g fresh cherries (or use good-quality tinned, drained weight)
juice of 1 lemon
50g caster sugar

For the white chocolate shard
300g white chocolate

HANDS-ON TIME:
1½ hours

HANDS-OFF TIME:
Freezing time for the ice cream

BAKING TIME:
35 minutes

SERVES:
8–10

SPECIAL EQUIPMENT:
23cm springclip cake tin, ice cream machine (optional), acetate sheets, kitchen thermometer, palette knife or scraper

METHOD USED:
Melting chocolate, page 24
Tempering chocolate, page 29

STORAGE:
The torte keeps for up to 5 days in the fridge

To make the ice cream

1. First make the **custard** for the ice cream. **Whisk** the egg yolks in a medium-sized bowl, just to break them up, and set to one side. Then heat the cream in a pan until it is hot, but not boiling. Slowly pour the hot cream over the egg yolks, whisking continuously to prevent them scrambling. Pour the egg and cream mixture back into the pan and let it cook gently, stirring continuously, for a good 10 minutes.

2. Put the white chocolate into the bowl that held the eggs, and when your custard in the pan has thickened slightly, pour it over the chocolate. Stir the contents of the bowl to melt the chocolate and mix it fully into the custard. Then put the mixture in the fridge to get fully cold, before whisking in the kirsch.

3. Freeze your ice cream. If you have an ice cream machine, it will churn the mixture as it freezes – follow the manufacturer's instructions and then transfer to a plastic container with a good airtight lid and store in the freezer until needed. To freeze ice cream without a machine, transfer the mixture to a wide plastic container with an airtight lid. You need the mixture to be no deeper than about 5cm, so you can beat it easily. Place in the freezer. After 1 hour remove the container and beat the mixture well, preferably with a hand-held electric mixer. Repeat this process twice more, at intervals of 1–1½ hours. Leave the ice cream in the freezer for at least 1 hour after the final beating, or until you are ready to serve. You can make the ice cream way ahead of time, as it will keep in the freezer for up to 3 months.

Continued

To make the pecan nut torte

4. Preheat the oven to 180°C (160°C fan), 350°F, Gas 4. Grease and **line** the base of your cake tin. Put the 200g butter and 200g chocolate into a small pan and **melt** them slowly over a low heat, stirring occasionally to mix them together.

5. Next put the 5 eggs and 200g sugar into a large bowl and whisk them well until they are light, fluffy and pale. Keep whisking as you pour in the melted chocolate mixture. Lastly fold in the 150g ground pecans and pinch of salt until you have a smooth batter.

6. Pour your cake batter into the prepared cake tin and bake it in the centre of the oven for 35 minutes. A skewer will not come out completely clean, as this is a moist cake. You will see some moist crumb, but if you still see lots of raw liquid mixture put the cake back in for 5 minutes. When the torte is done place it on a wire rack in its tin to cool completely.

To make the cherry compote

7. Put the 500g cherries into a small pan with the juice of 1 lemon and the 50g sugar. Bring the contents of the pan up to a simmer and then let it bubble until the cherries have softened and you have a thick sauce. It can be served hot or cold but when hot it contrasts well with the cold ice cream. If you want to make it ahead of time you can reheat it in the pan or microwave before serving.

To make the decorations

8. To make the decorations, **temper** some white chocolate. It is difficult to temper chocolate using much less than 300g, which will be more than you need for this recipe, so you may want to make the decorations when you are tempering chocolate for something else as well. The decorations will then keep in a cool place in an airtight container for several months.

Continued

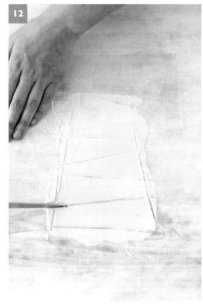

9. To temper your white chocolate, place 210g of it in a heatproof bowl set over a pan of simmering water. Using your kitchen thermometer, measure the temperature of the chocolate as it melts. Stir it to ensure the heat is evenly distributed and do not allow it to get above 40–45°C (104–113°F). Just before it is at the right temperature (as it is likely to continue to rise for a little while after you remove the heat source), take the bowl off the heat and continue to stir to melt any visible pieces of chocolate. Then add in the remaining 90g of chocolate and stir this into the melted chocolate. Keep stirring, as the newly added chocolate melts and the temperature comes down. Keep checking the temperature of the chocolate – you want it to reach 27°C (80.6°F). When it has come down to

the correct temperature, place the bowl back over the simmering water very briefly, keeping a watchful eye on the temperature. You want it to come back up to 30°C (86°F), but no higher. Bear in mind that the temperature will rise quickly, and continue to rise once you have removed the heat source.

10. When the white chocolate is at 30°C (86°F), leave the bowl off the heat and dip a knife into the molten chocolate to test if it has been successfully tempered. Scrape off one side on the edge of the bowl and allow the remaining chocolate to set in the fridge. Touch the set chocolate very lightly; if it feels smooth and dry and doesn't take the impression of your fingertip then it is tempered.

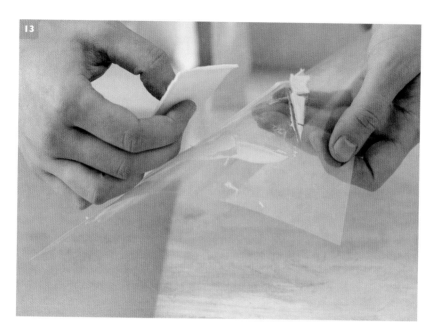

13

11. Lay acetate sheets onto a flat work surface ready to create your shards. When you have your bowl of tempered chocolate ready, work quickly as the longer you take, the thicker the chocolate will become as it cools. To create shards, use a palette knife or scraper to spread a fine layer of the chocolate on to your acetate sheets. Try not to overwork it but create the layer in one or two swift strokes. Then leave the chocolate for a few moments to firm up a little.

12. Next, with a knife, cut through the soft chocolate in sharp lines to create 8–10 create angular shard shapes (one for each serving).

13. Set all the finished chocolate sheets to one side to allow the chocolate to harden. When they are completely firm, break the chocolate up into the shards you have scored and place them on clean baking paper ready to serve or store.

To assemble
14. Remove the torte from the tin and cut into slices. Put a slice of the torte onto each serving plate, add a scoop of the white chocolate and kirsch ice cream and a spoonful of the compote, and lay a white chocolate shard across to give height.

What chocolate recipe shall I bake today?

Conversion Table

WEIGHT

Metric	Imperial
25g	1oz
50g	2oz
75g	2½oz
85g	3oz
100g	4oz
125g	4½oz
140g	5oz
175g	6oz
200g	7oz
225g	8oz
250g	9oz
280g	10oz
300g	11oz
350g	12oz
375g	13oz
400g	14oz
425g	15oz
450g	1lb
500g	1lb 2oz
550g	1lb 4oz
600g	1lb 5oz
650g	1lb 7oz
700g	1lb 9oz
750g	1lb 10oz
800g	1lb 12oz
850g	1lb 14oz
900g	2lb
950g	2lb 2oz
1kg	2lb 4oz

VOLUME

Metric	Imperial
30ml	1fl oz
50ml	2fl oz
75ml	3fl oz
125ml	4fl oz
150ml	¼ pint
175ml	6fl oz
200ml	7fl oz
225ml	8fl oz
300ml	½ pint
350ml	12fl oz
400ml	14fl oz
450ml	¾ pint
500ml	18fl oz
600ml	1 pint
725ml	1¼ pints
1 litre	1¾ pints

SPOON MEASURES

Metric	Imperial
5ml	1 teaspoon
10ml	2 teaspoons
15ml	1 tablespoon
30ml	2 tablespoons
45ml	3 tablespoons
60ml	4 tablespoons
75ml	5 tablespoons

LINEAR

Metric	Imperial
2.5cm	1in
3cm	1¼in
4cm	1½in
5cm	2in
5.5cm	2¼in
6cm	2½in
7cm	2¾in
7.5cm	3in
8cm	3¼in
9cm	3½in
9.5cm	3¾in
10cm	4in
11cm	4¼in
12cm	4½in
13cm	5in
14cm	5½in
15cm	6in
16cm	6½in
17cm	6½in
18cm	7in
19cm	7½in
20cm	8in
22cm	8½in
23cm	9in
24cm	9½in
25cm	10in

Index

Acknowledgements

Hodder & Stoughton and Love Productions would like to thank the following people for their contribution to this book:

Cat Black, Linda Collister, Laura Herring, Alasdair Oliver, Kate Brunt, Laura Oliver, Joanna Seaton, Sarah Christie, Alice Moore, Nicky Barneby, Anna Heath, Damian Horner, Auriol Bishop, Anna Beattie, Rupert Frisby, Jane Treasure, Claire Emerson.

The author would also like to thank Jenny, Jenni, Trish and Loulou, for testing, tasting and talking, thank you. Anthony and Zarrina, for teaching me to cook. Peter, Gideon and India May, for eating more chocolate than is strictly necessary.

First published in Great Britain in 2016
by Hodder & Stoughton
An Hachette UK company

1

Copyright © Love Productions Limited 2016
Photography & Design Copyright © Hodder & Stoughton Ltd 2016.

The right of Cat Black to be identified as the Author of the Work has been asserted by her in accordance with the Copyright, Designs and Patents Act 1988.

BBC and the BBC logo are trademarks of the British Broadcasting Corporation and are used under licence. BBC logo © BBC 1996.

A CIP catalogue record for this title is available from the British Library

Hardback ISBN 9781473615489
Ebook ISBN 9781473615496

Editorial Director: Nicky Ross
Editor: Sarah Hammond
Project Editor: Laura Herring
Series Editor: Linda Collister
Art Director & Designer: Alice Moore
Photographer: Matt Russell, Rita Platts
Food Stylist: Jack Sargeson
Props Stylist: Lydia Brun

Typeset in Dear Joe, Mostra, Kings Caslon and Gill Sans
Printed and bound in Italy by L.E.G.O. Spa

Hodder & Stoughton policy is to use papers that are natural, renewable and recyclable products and made from wood grown in sustainable forests. The logging and manufacturing processes are expected to conform to the environmental regulations of the country of origin.

Hodder & Stoughton Ltd
Carmelite House
50 Victoria Embankment
London EC4Y 0DZ

www.hodder.co.uk

Continue on your journey to star baker with tips
and advice on how to *Bake It Better* from the
GREAT BRITISH BAKE OFF team.

DON'T JUST BAKE. BAKE IT BETTER.